# Flax

## The
## Super Food

Barbara Bloomfield,
Judy Brown,
Siegfried Gursche

Book Publishing Company
Summertown, Tennessee

Cover design: Warren Jefferson, Cynthia Holzapfel
Interior design: Michael Cook

Published in the United States by
Book Publishing Company
P.O. Box 99
Summertown, TN 38483
888-260-8458
http://www.bookpubco.com

03 02 01 00     1 2 3 4 5 6

ISBN: 1-57067-099-4

Bloomfield, Barb
 Flax the super food: delicious recipes for better health / Barbara Bloomfield, Siegfried Gursche, Judy Brown.
      p. cm.
 Includes index.
 ISBN 1-57067-099-4 (alk. paper)
  1. Flaxseed in human nutrition. I. Gursche, Siegfried. II. Brown, Judy A. III. Title.
 QP144.O44 B565 2000
 613.2'84--dc21                                        00-024071

Calculations for the nutritional analyses in this book are based on the average number of servings listed with the recipes and the average amount of an ingredient, if a range is called for. Calculations are rounded up to the nearest gram. If two options for an ingredient are listed, the first one is used. Not included are optional ingredients, serving suggestions, or fat used for frying, unless the amount of fat is specified in the recipe.

# Contents

# Flax
## The Super Food

# *Flax*

## *A Super-Healing Food*

Flax is a nutritional powerhouse and a super-healing food. It is an ancient but little-known seed whose benefits have only recently been recognized in North America by nutritionists, dietitians, and naturopathic doctors. Even in orthodox medical circles it has gained attention and is now being studied as a "nutraceutical": a food with many nutrients and pharmaceutical properties. The empirical evidence, which for thousands of years has shown flax to be a healing food, has recently been substantiated in clinical studies at universities and hospitals around the world. For example, the University of Toronto recently published results of studies conducted by Dr. Stephen Cunnane which showed that flax lowers blood cholesterol levels.[1] Studies by Serraino and Thompson, show that flax prevents the growth of new cancer cells.[2] At a recent convention on experimental biology, the American Food and Drug Agency endorsed flaxseeds as a food for disease prevention. Without a doubt, flax has a promising future and a great place in human nutrition as a healing food and nutraceutical. Everyone could benefit by adding flaxseeds to their diet, especially those who suffer from constipation, intestinal and digestive problems, high blood pressure, elevated cholesterol levels, and cardiovascular and other degenerative diseases. Flax is reasonably priced and is an affordable addition to the daily diet, even for the budget-minded consumer.

My first encounter with flax (or linseed as we called it at that time) was when I was eleven. I spent a summer and fall with my grandfather on his small farm in eastern Germany. He had about thirty-six acres of land, with four cows, two horses, a flock of geese, ducks, and chickens. It was 1944, the year before World War II ended. Food was generally scarce and farmers tried to be self-sufficient by growing a wide variety of foods, including potatoes, vegetables, all kinds of grains—barley, rye, and wheat for baking their own bread and oats for the horses—

and flax. I still remember the field of blue flax in bloom the day I arrived at the farm. It was an unforgettable sight.

Farmers grew flax for several reasons. The fiber of the plant stems was processed and spun into a yarn used for weaving fine linen, hence the name linseed. My grandmother loved to work with flax fiber. The strands of fiber were very long, and she spun them on her simple spinning wheel into a thin and even thread that was much finer than wool. To this day, fine linen tablecloths, sheets, and clothes are treasured for their beauty, texture, and durability.

Farmers know how to use flaxseeds to treat many diseases and keep their animals healthy. So do veterinarians. My father, who grew up on this small farm, was responsible for brushing the horses. He observed that flax-fed horses had much shinier coats than those that didn't, and this made his job easier.

Flax is a boon to farmers for other reasons as well. The small, hard brown seeds soak up eight times their weight in water. Nature has made it that way so that the kernel, when seeded, can store enough moisture to sprout and grow, even if there is a lengthy dry spell after the first rain. In the midwest of the U.S. and in Canada, Australia, and eastern Europe (where most of the world's flax is grown today), farmers often face dry spells after the seed has been put into the ground without worrying whether their flax will sprout.

I remember one day my grandfather rushed into the storage room with a bucket of hot water, grabbed a few handfuls of flaxseeds, and mixed them into the water. "There is trouble with the cow," he said. "I let her out of the barn too early after the rain, and she ate too much wet grass." (Cows who eat large amounts of wet grass will experience bloating.) "This flax will fix her in no time! All that's needed is that the seeds soak up the water in the next half hour." And sure enough, within half an hour the flax and water turned into a warm slurry mash which the cow slurped up happily.

This ability of the kernels to soak up an incredible amount of water and turn it into mucilage (a gelatinous liquid) has also provided mankind with gentle relief from all kinds of gastrointestinal discomfort, congestion, and constipation for thousands of years. Flax mucilage is an excellent remedy for stomach ulcers, as it covers the inflamed areas and protects them from stomach acids. Because flax is very alkaline, it also helps to prevent heartburn and should be included in all detoxification programs to restore the body's proper acid-alkaline balance.

There are many more wonderful things to be said about flax. Some you may already know; others may be new to you. While the facts about flax are no longer secret, the many health benefits are still widely unknown.

## Flaxseeds—Food or Drug?

Flax is an oil-bearing seed. It contains the highest percentage of both essential fats, (linolenic or omega-3, and linoleic or omega-6) of any oil-bearing seed. These fats are necessary for the proper functioning of many organs. They are not produced by the body, however, so they must be supplied by the diet. These are the healing fats Udo Erasmus talks about in detail in his book *Fats that Heal, Fats that Kill* (Alive Books, Vancouver, Canada). The main purpose of these two essential fatty acids is not to provide energy or to store fat in the body. Instead, they are meant to supply the body with hormone-like substances called prostaglandins and eicosanoids, which ensure the proper functioning of the brain, nervous system, skin, and sexual organs. They help to control high blood pressure by thinning the blood and preventing the formation of blood clots. Essential fatty acids also increase metabolism and encourage the body to burn more fat. The scientist H.M. Sinclair reported in 1984 that after putting himself on an experimental diet high in omega-3, he noticed striking changes in his body. First he lost weight (wow!), his energy level increased, and he experienced more vitality than ever! Dr. Johanna Budwig, a pioneer in the field of health and nutrition research, explains that flax oil is the "spark plug" that cranks up fat metabolism in our bodies.[3] There are many other health benefits of flaxseeds that will be covered a little later in this book.

## *Flax Has a Long History*

Flaxseeds have been part of the human diet for over 5,000 years. Records tell us that in ancient Babylon (3000 BC) flax was already cultivated for food. One thousand years later, a complex irrigation system was developed along the Euphrates and Tigris rivers, mainly to ensure a rich harvest of flax.

The famed Greek physician Hippocrates (460-377 BC), father of natural medicine, recognized flax as a food which relieves intestinal discomfort. He coined the often quoted, now proverbial phrase, "Let food be your medicine and your medicine be your food." There is probably no better commodity than flax that fits both categories: food and medicine.

Charlemagne (742-814 AD) King of the Franks and Holy Roman Emperor, established laws in his medical law book *Capitulare*, governing the cultivation of flax for food and medicinal purposes. Because of the unique properties of flaxseeds, their high nutrient and fiber content, he considered them of utmost importance as cleansers and relievers of gastrointestinal problems.

Flax is not native to North America. It was brought to Quebec in 1617 by Canadian farmer Lois Hebert. Throughout the centuries, flax has been widely used in Europe as a staple food. The seeds store well and provide good nourishment in lean times. Today, you will have a hard time finding any bakery in Germany that does not bake a flax-rye bread. The oil from the flaxseeds adds moisture to the bread, thereby extending its shelf-life and improving its texture. Whenever I travel to Germany, I'm astonished to see the variety of breads and buns baked with flax. The Flax Council of Canada reports that in Germany over 60,000 tons of flaxseed are consumed annually in bread and cereal. On average, that amounts to about one kilogram per person per year or three grams (one teaspoon) daily. Current consumption levels of flaxseed by Canadians are low enough that Statistics Canada does not yet document them as it does many other, more common foods. However, the stage is set for a change.

## *Mucilage*

Why does flax work so well as a laxative? It all has to do with the hard shell which makes up twelve percent of the seed. As soon as this shell comes in contact with moisture, it absorbs that moisture quickly and expands into a gelatinous liquid known as mucilage. Two tablespoons of flaxseed stirred into a glass of boiling hot water will thicken up quickly and have the consistency of a pudding. To use flax as a laxative, drink the mix before it thickens up—the thickening will then happen in the stomach. If constipation persists, drink a glass of water with thirty grams of whole flaxseeds (two tablespoons) twice daily before meals. By the way, the unbroken flaxseed, protected by the shell, will pass right through the digestive system without breaking down. For our bodies to digest flaxseeds and benefit from their many nutritional qualities, including the oils, the shell or hull must be broken.

The flax mucilage can also serve another important purpose, namely to repair the damage caused by taking massive doses of antibiotics. The friendly bacteria in your intestines are destroyed in large quantities if you take antibiotics, birth control pills, or other drugs, particularly over a long period of time, and chronic constipation (common among hospital patients) may develop. Flax mucilage helps the intestinal flora to re-establish itself. German author Dr. Ernst Schneider (*Take Advantage of the Healing Power of Nutrition*, Saatkorn-Verlag, 1985) agrees:

"From my previous experience, the intestinal flora recovers more quickly from a chemotherapeutic shock if freshly crushed flax is consumed regularly. The mucilage from flax helps to repair any damage to the internal wallpaper, which is the coating of mucus that lines the entire digestive tract. Even people who suffer from stomach ulcers will heal better and faster by eating flax because the mucilage covers the inflamed areas and protects them from the stomach acids."

# Fiber

Sixty years ago, scientists began to study the effects of food fiber on human health and discovered why flax was so successful as a laxative. At first, scientists believed that fiber had no nutritional value and was therefore unimportant or useless in any food or diet. That is why bran (which is all fiber) was removed from the grain in the milling process, leaving behind only white, starchy flour stripped of all vitamins and minerals. Then researchers began looking at the diets of people who lived in underdeveloped countries. These people typically ate high-fiber diets and did not experience constipation and other kinds of intestinal disorders, like Crohn's disease, diverticulitis, and high cholesterol, which are rampant in all industrialized nations. Suddenly, fiber became a medical buzzword. In flaxseeds, fiber is the structural material of the shells and the substance in which the oil is embedded. Humans cannot digest it, but the friendly bacteria or micro-organisms thriving in the intestines can, and they use it for energy.

Like many other foods, flax has two types of fiber: soluble and insoluble. Two-thirds of the fiber in flax is insoluble, consisting of cellulose and lignin. This fiber cleans out the intestines like a broom, reducing bowel transit time by forcing fecal matter to be expelled rapidly. The other one-third of fiber is water soluble and plays an important role in reducing serum cholesterol levels and regulating blood glucose levels. This is good news for people with diabetes. The British Journal of Nutrition confirmed these positive effects on persons consuming flaxseeds daily during a four-week study.[4] The blood glucose levels of the people in the study group were reduced by twenty-seven percent, while their cholesterol levels were reduced by seven percent. In all cases their bowel movements improved. This is important because fecal matter that lingers in the intestines creates harmful compounds and toxins. This can cause serious illness and even cancer of the colon. In fact, the National Cancer Institute has officially recognized fiber as an important element in the diet for the prevention of many cancers.

## *Lignans*

Not too long ago the words "lignin" or "lignan" could not be found in any medical dictionary. Lignans are an important, newly discovered group of substances. They are plant estrogens (phytoestrogens) that may play a key role in the prevention of breast, prostate, uterine, and colon cancers. These friendly plant hormones not only prevent some cancers but they also play an important role in maintaining healthy, strong bones. Lignans also prevent the formation of gallstones by binding with bile acids. According to the research of Dr. L. Thompson of the University of Toronto, flaxseeds are the richest source of lignans and contain 75 to 800 times more than 66 other plant foods tested, including wheat bran, oats, millet, rye, legumes, and soybeans.[5]

Lignans also protect the body from estrogen-driven cancers by expelling excess estrogen from the body and by interfering with tumor cell growth. It is a well-established fact that Mexican, Japanese, and Chinese women whose diet is high in fiber and lignans, are far less likely to develop breast cancer than women eating the standard North American diet. What is more, lignans attach themselves to estrogen receptor sites and take the place of estradiol and estrone, which are implicated in breast cancer. Lignans also inhibit estrogen production from fatty tissue. Many studies support the contention that people who consume high amounts of flax with lignans are able to balance the hormone levels in their body.

Furthermore, researchers believe that lignans may help treat or prevent heart disease, diabetes, high blood pressure, and possibly asthma. Finally, lignans have anti-bacterial, anti-viral, and anti-fungal properties, and this makes flax a powerful immune system booster.

## *The Wonder Grain*

Flaxseed has some additional healthful ingredients, which makes it an excellent complete food for humans. It contains vitamins A, B1, B2, C, D, and E, plus a full array of minerals and trace minerals, carotene, lecithin, and phospholipids. The seed contains 35 to 45% oil, 12% fiber, 10% mucilage, and 22% protein. It should be noted that the composition varies from one variety of seed to another and is dependent on climatic conditions. For example, one growing season may have ideal weather conditions yielding a perfect crop, while a rainy and cold summer may produce meager seeds. Flax is the ideal survival food. Everything is well protected within a hard shell that contains antioxidants (such as vitamins C, E, and beta carotene) that will keep the seed fresh for many years. Only when the shell is broken and the oil is exposed to oxygen will the oil spoil and go rancid.

## *Interesting Discoveries*

In the late '70s and early '80s, I was involved in extensive research for the development of marketable flax products, including a stable cracked flaxseed and cold-pressed, unrefined fresh flax oil. I was traveling the Canadian prairies meeting with flax growers. In Vulcan, south of Calgary, I met Russel Smith, an organic farmer cultivating many acres of flax. We looked at all popular varieties of brown flax—about six different kinds. It was here that I saw for the first time three different kinds of golden (or yellow) flax. The kernels of the golden flax were generally larger, slightly softer, and, in my opinion, tastier than the brown ones.

Russel explained that golden flax is usually a little more expensive than brown flax. The reason is that the harvest yield per acre is much less than for brown flax. Golden flax has a higher protein content, but it does not yield as much oil. That is why yellow flax was not used for pressing oils, but for making cereals and baking bread. He informed me that plant breeders in Manitoba who were involved in a cooperative agreement with Agriculture Canada were experimenting with yellow flax to increase the oil content with very little omega-3 in it. Australian plant breeders had already developed a genetically modified variety of yellow flax with dramatically reduced levels of omega-3 in order to enhance its resistance to oxidation. The aim of this project was to create a strain of flax which would not turn rancid, thereby extending its shelf-life and making it suitable as a cooking oil.

In May 1993, Health and Welfare Canada gave its approval to market refined Linola™ oil in Canada, which is an oil produced from the seeds of this genetically engineered seed. Here is another example of industry, motivated by financial gain, tinkering with nature in order to produce an oil where the most nutritious ingredient (omega-3) was eliminated. While the shelf-life of this product is extended, it will not extend the span of a human life.

The original unmodified golden seeds we worked with are very nutritious and today are used mostly as cereal. To be used this way, the seeds needed to be processed in such a way that the stomach juices can penetrate the seeds and digest them without opening the oil cells. They needed to be intact to avoid oxygenation and rancidity. In our experiments, golden flax was most suitable when crushed slightly, not cracked or milled—just squeezed enough to crack the shell open without damaging the oil cells. In this way, the kernels could be used as ready-made cereal, sprinkled on hot cereal, and absorb liquids without the oil turning rancid. We coined this edible golden flax product "Linoseed," which I personally prefer to brown flax for breakfast muesli. Milled flax or flax meal from brown flax, loosely packaged in plastic bags, used to be very popular in the 1970s and is still sold in some health food stores today. Dr. Paavo Airola, Canada's leading nutritionist at that time, warned consumers not to purchase flax meal or ground flax, as the exposed oil in ground flax oxidizes rapidly and goes rancid within days. Heat, light, and air all contribute to this process of rapid oxidization. Rancid oils should be avoided because they are toxic and cancer-causing. Today, however, some companies offer specially milled flaxseeds in vacuum-sealed foil packages. They utilize a unique new milling technique and can guarantee freshness. If you would like to try these products, make sure that the production date is no more than three months before the purchase date and once the package is opened, refrigerate it, keep the bag tightly closed, and consume it within two weeks.

Another interesting discovery we made was that varieties of flax grown in colder regions, such as Saskatchewan or the

Peace River region in northern Alberta, contain proportionally more omega-3 linolenic fatty acids and less omega-6 linoleic fatty acids than varieties grown in warmer climates, such as the midwestern United States. This phenomenon was also reflected in the taste, as flax produced in a colder climate has a slightly bitter and stronger flavor.

It is fortunate that plants in these northern climates have adapted to produce more omega-3 in their oils, which stay liquid even in freezing temperatures. Oil seeds, like sunflower or safflower grown in warmer regions have only traces of omega-3, while sesame, almond, or olive oil, as well as all tropical oils, such as coconut, palm, avocado, macadamia, and brazil nut oils, have no omega-3 at all. Yet people living in the tropics consuming tropical oils without omega-3 and little omega-6 still do well without showing any symptoms of fat-related degenerative diseases. The secret is obviously that populations living in the tropics consume their coconut and palm oils in unrefined, natural states. Once these people adopt a diet including refined, heat-damaged vegetable oils, they show the same symptoms of degenerative diseases that are rampant in industrialized nations.

Flax has so much to offer! It is unequaled in versatility as a therapeutic plant and as a nourishing food. As a matter of fact, flaxseeds could be called the Golden Miracle Workers. Consider them when you are thinking about your health and that of your family.

## *Endnotes*

1. SC Cunnane et al., "High alpha-linolenic acid flaxseed: some nutritional properties in humans," *British Journal of Nutrition* 69:443.

2. M Serraino and LU Thompson, "The effect of flaxseed supplementation on the initiation and promotional stages of mammary tumorogenesis," *Nutr. Cancer* 17:153.

3. Johanna Budwig, *Flax Oil As a True Aid Against Arthritis, Heart Infarction, Cancer and Other Diseases* (Vancouver: Apple Publishing, 1994).

4. See note 1 above.

5. LU Thompson et al., "Mammalian lignan production from various foods," *Nutr. Cancer 16:43.*

## *Flax oil*

It just wouldn't be right to talk about all the health benefits of flaxseeds and not mention the oils pressed from flaxseeds. Flax oil is in a class of its own, simply because it is the only oil that is made up almost entirely of very good poly-unsaturated essential fatty acids. Essential means that the fatty acids are

---

### Benefits of Eating Flaxseeds and Oil

| Biochemical Effect | Clinical Result |
|---|---|
| Normalizes the body's fatty acids | Smoother skin, shiny hair, soft hands increased stamina, vitality, and agility |
| Normalizes and rebalances prostaglandins | Smoother muscle action improvement of many other functions |
| Reduces appetite provocation | Eliminates bingeing or addictive need for food |
| Stabilizes insulin and blood sugar | Keeps stamina high for long level periods |
| Strengthens the immune system | Avoids or overcomes food allergies fights off some diseases more effectively |
| Increases fiber and aerobic bacteria | Promotes proper functioning of the bacteria in the digestive tract to avoid gas, constipation and other disorders |
| Normalizes blood fats and lowers cholesterol | Stronger cardiovascular system: clear thinking |
| Corrects the body's thermogenic system | Burns off fat increased (ability to burn off calories) cold-weather resistance increases comfort |
| Elevates the level of estrogen in blood | Dramatically reduces many post-menopausal discomforts in post-menopausal women |
| Supports liver in fat metabolism | Lowers or normalizes blood pressure |

Adapted from *The Omega 3 Phenomenon* by Donald O. Rudin, MD and Clara Felix, 1996 (Avery Publishing, Garden City Park, NY)

---

required by the body to stay healthy, and they need to come from food sources because the body cannot produce them on its own. Polyunsaturated oils are hungry for oxygen, and this is the reason why they go rancid so quickly. They also dry quickly, which is why linseed oil is used for paint.

Flaxseed contains 42 percent oil. When expeller pressed in a cold process, the yield is about 33 percent oil. This oil is made up of 48 to 64 percent linolenic fatty acids (omega-3) which makes flax the richest plant source of this nutrient. Sixteen to 34 percent is linoleic fatty acids (omega-6) and the balance (18 percent) is mostly oleic fatty acids (omega-9), a monounsaturated, nonessential fatty acid mostly found in olive oil.

Since flax oil is polyunsaturated, with the main component being omega-3, it spoils quickly when heated or exposed to oxygen and light. You'll want to use it for cold dishes only, in salad dressings for all kinds of green salads, potato salad, grated carrot salad, coleslaw, or with raw sauerkraut. Freshly pressed, unrefined flax oil is delicious when poured over a baked potato with some herbal salt. I love it.

The great comeback of flax oil was initiated by Dr. Johanna Budwig with her famous oil-protein diet for cancer patients and others suffering from cardiovascular disease, arthritis, and other degenerative diseases. The recipe consisted mainly of flax oil mixed into quark (a soft, spreadable cheese made by straining warmed kefir, yogurt, or buttermilk), a grated apple, and freshly ground flaxseeds.

I visited Dr. Johanna Budwig on two occasions while traveling in Germany. She was a a pioneering scientist in the field of health and nutrition and a fascinating person to talk with.

Her greatest contribution was the isolation and identification of fatty substances in the blood. She was the first scientist to analyze the different fatty acids through gas and paper chromophotography, making it possible to determine good fats from bad fats. Dr. Budwig exposed the margarine manufacturers' methods of turning nutritious unrefined oils into highly processed and hydrogenated health-endangering margarine.

She maintained that the process of artificially hardening liquid vegetable oils (hydrogenation) creates life-threatening fat molecules—trans-fatty acids. The orthodox medical establishment, margarine manufacturers, and the government all opposed her in one way or another and attempted to suppress her findings by prosecuting her for claiming that trans-fatty acids and the hydrogenation process are harmful to humans. The margarine industry took her to court. She fought twenty-eight court cases in her life and won all of them. Today, it is widely accepted that trans-fatty acids are the cause of certain cancers, heart disease, and many other degenerative diseases.

Dr. Budwig concluded that fresh unrefined flax oil had the best health-giving profile provided it was not heated. Heating flax oil and other polyunsaturated fats turns the good cis form of the fatty acids into the bad trans form.

When choosing flax oil, or any edible oil for that matter, be very, very careful. Not all manufacturers offer a high-quality product and deliver what the label promises. Before I was involved in setting up an oil pressing plant in Vancouver, my wife and I traveled to Europe and visited Dr. Budwig and a number of oil mills, where so-called cold-pressed oils were produced. We visited East Germany's most productive flax oil mill in Halberstadt. We also saw the old oil mill in Künzelsau and looked at a great number of modern oil presses. What we saw was not encouraging. Neither were we impressed with the large volume oil pressers in Saskatoon or San Francisco. They all used huge, outdated platen or expeller presses which produced considerable high heat in the pressing process. The oil they produced was unpalatable and in need of further refining. Their labels, however, read cold-pressed or expeller-pressed, always hiding the fact that the oil was refined. The government does not require manufacturers to declare on the label that an oil has been refined. Yet the refining process requires a high temperature which changes the molecular structure of flax oil from the cis to the trans form.

We wanted to produce truly cold-pressed, unrefined, fresh-tasting flax oil and found the suitable presses in Germany. Of course, they operated slowly and could press only small amounts, but they made delicious unrefined flax oil. With the proper packaging and bottling equipment (which would keep light and oxygen out), our company was the first to supply North America with true, fresh cold-pressed and unrefined flax oil. Today, there are at least six reliable companies in Canada and the U.S. that press the oil the way we did, and the result is a variety of healthful healing oils for the consumer.

The label information you need to look for is a statement including the words "cold expeller-pressed" and most importantly, "unrefined." You should also see a pressing date; do not purchase flax oil after six months past the pressing date. Rather, buy 250 ml bottles and consume the oil within three weeks after opening rather than buying larger bottles just to save money. One more thing: beware of supermarket oils. Other than extra-virgin and virgin olive oils and those just mentioned, all oils are refined, heat-treated, and contain dangerous trans-fatty acids. At present, the government does not require oil manufacturers to declare the percentage of trans-fatty acids on the label, but may do so in the future. Once vegetable oils have undergone the heat refining process, heat-damaged fat molecules (trans-fatty acids) are present.

## Tip

Always purchase unrefined oils. Make sure they are packaged in dark containers, as light will damage oils. You will find these oils in the refrigerator section of natural food stores.

It is unfortunate, however, that some natural food stores continue to sell unrefined oils in clear glass bottles. These products offer no advantage over refined oils.

## How to Use Flax

Most natural food stores carry flaxseeds, which are sometimes packaged on the premises. It is most economical to purchase flax in bulk and store the seeds in canisters at home in a dry place. The most common are the smaller, shiny reddish-brown seeds. They are flat and oval with pointed tips, slightly larger than sesame seeds, and have a nutty flavor. Some stores also carry the golden or yellow variety or may stock them for you upon request. These seeds are slightly larger and a little softer, making them perfect for cereal.

The best way to integrate flax into your diet is in its raw form. The recommended portion is one tablespoon (15 grams or ½ ounce) per day. For grinding the seeds, I recommend obtaining an electric coffee grinder, like those made by Braun, Salton, or Philips. They can be bought anywhere for under $20 and do a wonderful job grinding the seeds. Do not attempt to grind flax in a regular flour mill. With their high oil content, the seeds, will quickly plug up the grinding stones. A blender would work also, but it's rather big for a small job. Using an electric coffee grinder, pulse the seeds for just two seconds—not longer. This turns the seeds into a coarse powder, ready to use. You can stir the flax powder into cooked multi-grain cereal or yogurt. There are many other ways to use freshly ground raw flax which you will find in the recipe section. Eating flaxseeds raw will provide you with the total food value including the protein and the health benefits of the essential fats and lignans.

As mentioned earlier, flax is a highly effective laxative. In order to use it in this way, measure two tablespoons of flax per one cup of water. If you use warm water, you can just stir the seeds in and drink the mixture on an empty stomach upon rising or immediately before meals. If you prefer, you can use apple juice or any other liquid you like, stir the seeds in, and wait for half an hour until they have soaked up the liquid, and then eat it with a spoon.

You can even derive benefits from cooked flaxseeds. All you have to do is to add one or two tablespoons of seeds to two or three cups of water and bring the mixture to a boil. Remove immediately, strain the mucilage, then mix it into soups, sauces, or vegetable or grain dishes. Naturally, a few spoonfuls of ground seeds can be added to vegetable broth to thicken it or make a soup more creamy. Keep in mind not to boil ground flax; just add the ground flax after the boiling soup has been removed from the heat and let stand for five minutes before serving. For soups, I actually like the ground golden flax—it looks better. I have a vegan friend who soaks flaxseeds in water, stirs them through a strainer, and uses the gel in recipes whenever eggs are called for. There are several other tasty ways flaxseeds can be used, and these are listed in the recipe section.

As mentioned earlier, flax can be used in baking bread, buns, and muffins. I have often been asked, "What about the heat—doesn't it harm the omega-3s and -6s?" This is certainly a valid question and the answer is no, the essential fats will be unharmed. As you may remember from your high school chemistry class, the temperature of water does not rise beyond 212°F, unless under pressure. In other words, the water absorbed by the seeds keeps the oil from overheating. When you bake bread, you can replace ten to thirty percent of the wheat flour with flax meal. As the proportion of ground flaxseed increases, the baked volume decreases, resulting in a firmer loaf.

Finally, flaxseeds can work for you on the outside. Externally, cracked flax makes a very good poultice for sore and bruised muscles as well as inflamed tissues. The poultice also brings relief for rheumatic pains and neuralgia. Skin conditions such as wounds, boils, ulcerations, and inflammations benefit from repeated flax poultice applications. Internal inflammations, such as bursitis, gastric inflammation, cystitis, and kidney and gall stone formation can be alleviated by regularly applying a poultice. It's easy to make. Simply grind three or four tablespoons flaxseeds, then transfer the flax meal into a dish. Pour a large cup of boiling water over the ground flax, let steep for ten minutes, and spread the warm paste onto a large handkerchief or similar cloth. Fold the cloth to cover the warm paste, then apply to the affected area and wrap with a thick towel.

Flaxseeds can even be helpful in skin-cleansing programs and are especially effective on oily, blemished skin. Young people with problem skin will find this to be much more helpful than relying on harsh chemical compounds. To make the mildly abrasive skin cleanser, mix equal parts of freshly ground flaxseeds and wheat bran. Take two tablespoons of the mixture, and stir in enough hot water to make a paste. Moisten your face with water, then gently massage the skin with the mix in a circular motion. This cleansing stimulates the circulation and leaves the skin feeling soft and smooth.

# Flax–The Super Food

# Breakfast

# *Scrambled Tofu*

### Yield: 3 servings

*Jazz up this delicious breakfast basic with sautéed onions, mushrooms, bell peppers, fried potato chunks or rice, or top with shredded soy cheese.*

**2 teaspoons minced garlic**
**½ teaspoon canola oil**
**1 pound firm tofu, mashed with a fork or potato masher**
**1 tablespoon tamari**
**¼ teaspoon turmeric**
**2 tablespoons nutritional yeast**
**2 tablespoons ground flaxseeds**

In a medium skillet, brown the minced garlic in the canola oil.

Add the tofu, tamari, and turmeric while stirring. Cook for 2 to 3 minutes until the tofu is very hot, but keep it moist. Just before you're ready to turn off the heat, add the nutritional yeast and ground flaxseeds. Stir well and remove from the heat. Cover until ready to serve.

Per serving: Calories 163, Protein 14 g, Fat 10 g, Carbohydrates 7 g, Fiber 2 g

# *Hash Browns*

**Yield: 2 to 3 servings**

*Mix in crumbled firm tofu before cooking the grated pota-toes to make a high-protein breakfast treat.*

**3 cups grated potatoes**
**¾ cup chopped onions**
**½ teaspoon olive oil**
**2 tablespoons ground flaxseeds**
**Salt and pepper, to taste**

Rinse the grated potatoes in a bowl of cold water. This will wash out a lot of the starch. Pour into a colander to drain off the water.

In a medium skillet, start to brown the onions in the olive oil. Add the potatoes and cook while stirring occasionally until they are crispy and browned. Add the ground flaxseeds, salt, and pepper. Stir well, remove from the heat, and serve while hot.

Per serving: Calories 213, Protein 4 g, Fat 5 g, Carbohydrates 44 g, Fiber 6 g

# *Pancakes*

### Yield: Twelve 4-inch pancakes

*Pancakes are the easiest way to get flax into your children's breakfasts without them ever knowing it.*

**1 cup unbleached white flour**
**1 cup whole wheat pastry flour**
**2 teaspoons baking powder**
**¼ teaspoon salt**
**3 tablespoons ground flaxseeds**
**2 tablespoons canola oil**
**2 cups nondairy milk**

Mix the flours, baking powder, salt, and ground flaxseeds together in a medium mixing bowl. Make a well in the center, and add the oil and milk. Stir thoroughly but leave a few lumps. Cook on a lightly oiled skillet for 2 to 3 minutes on each side until golden brown.

Per pancake: Calories 108, Protein 4 g, Fat 4 g, Carbohydrates 15 g, Fiber 2 g

# *Waffles*

### Yield: 5 waffles

*These are good topped with soy yogurt and fresh fruit.*

**1½ tablespoons flaxseeds**
**½ cup warm water**

*Liquid ingredients*

**1½ cups soymilk**
**½ cup water**
**2 tablespoons canola oil**

*Dry ingredients*

**1 cup unbleached white flour**
**⅔ cup whole wheat flour**
**⅓ cup cornmeal**
**¼ teaspoon salt**
**2 teaspoons baking powder**

Preheat a waffle iron.

Process the flaxseeds with the warm water in a blender until the consistency is smooth and creamy and the seeds are broken up into small, dark flecks. Combine with the liquid ingredients, and set aside.

In a medium mixing bowl, combine the dry ingredients. Make a well in the dry ingredients, and pour in the liquid ingredients. Stir until all the dry ingredients are absorbed. Don't beat or mix more than necessary.

Ladle out a scoop of batter onto a lightly oiled, preheated waffle iron.

Only the first batch needs oil; the rest shouldn't stick. If they begin to stick, use a little more oil. Cook the waffles until they begin to turn brown but are still soft.

Per waffle: Calories 252, Protein 7 g, Fat 8 g, Carbohydrates 37 g, Fiber 5 g

# *French Toast*

Yield: 6 slices

*The combination of ground flaxseeds and nutritional yeast flakes makes the perfect egg substitute for this breakfast favorite.*

**⅔ cup soymilk**
**¼ cup nutritional yeast flakes**
**1 tablespoon ground flaxseeds blended with ⅓ cup water**
**⅛ teaspoon salt**
**⅛ teaspoon cinnamon**
**6 slices of whole wheat bread**

In a medium mixing bowl, whip the soymilk, nutritional yeast, ground flaxseed and water mixture, salt, and cinnamon.

Dip the each slice of bread into the soymilk mixture. Turn over with a fork so both sides are saturated. In a lightly oiled skillet, cook 3 minutes on each side. Serve with maple syrup.

Per slice: Calories 81, Protein 5 g, Fat 2 g, Carbohydrates 11 g, Fiber 3 g

# *Biscuits*

### Yield: 12 biscuits

*If you must eat breakfast on the run, there's nothing better than one of these biscuits with a slice of breaded, oven-fried tofu in the middle.*

### Liquid ingredients

1½ tablespoons flaxseeds
½ cup warm water
¼ cup oil
1 cup soymilk

### Dry ingredients

1 cup whole wheat flour
2 cups unbleached flour
¼ teaspoon salt
2 teaspoons baking powder

Preheat the oven to 425°F.

Process the flaxseeds with the warm water in a blender until the consistency is smooth and creamy and the seeds are broken up into small, dark flecks. Combine with the remaining liquid ingredients, and set aside.

In a medium mixing bowl, combine the dry ingredients and mix well. Add to the liquid ingredients, and mix until a stiff dough is formed.

Press the dough out onto a well-floured surface. Sprinkle flour over the dough, and press with your hands to make ½ inch thick. Cut out biscuits with a large biscuit cutter, and place them on a cookie sheet. Bake for 12 minutes.

Per biscuit: Calories 141, Protein 4 g, Fat 5 g, Carbohydrates 20 g, Fiber 2 g

# *Banana Smoothie*

### Yield: 2 cups

*Make a great pineapple-banana smoothie by replacing the soymilk, yogurt, and vanilla with 1 cup each orange juice and pineapple juice and adding to the remaining ingredients.*

**1 cup vanilla soymilk**
**2 frozen bananas**
**½ cup vanilla soy yogurt**
**2 tablespoons freshly squeezed lemon juice**
**1 teaspoon vanilla**
**2 teaspoons flax oil**
**2 pitted dates**
**3 to 4 ice cubes**

Blend together the soymilk, bananas, yogurt, lemon juice, vanilla, flax oil, and dates until smooth.

Add the ice cubes and blend until smooth.

Serve immediately, or pour into popsicle molds and freeze.

*Variation: Add fresh strawberries, peaches, nectarines, etc.*

Per cup: Calories 233, Protein 5 g, Fat 9 g, Carbohydrates 34 g, Fiber 5 g

# Flax–The Super Food

# Breads

# Whole Wheat Bread

### Yield: 2 loaves, 12 slices each

*This is one of the most traditional ways to incorporate flax into your daily diet.*

**3 cups lukewarm water**
**1 tablespoon baking yeast**
**¼ cup sugar or liquid sweetener**
**2 cups unbleached white flour**
**3 tablespoons canola oil**
**1 teaspoon salt**
**½ cup ground flaxseeds**
**3 to 4 cups whole wheat flour**

In a medium mixing bowl, make a sponge by beating together the water, yeast, sweetener, and 2 cups of flour. Let rest for 10 minutes until bubbly.

Add the oil, salt, flaxseeds, and 3 cups of the whole wheat flour. Mix with a wooden spoon until the flour has been absorbed. Turn out onto a floured surface, and knead for 5 to 10 minutes until satiny smooth. Add more flour if the dough sticks to your hands.

Lightly oil the bowl and put the dough back into it. Let it rise in a warm place until almost doubled in bulk. Divide the dough into 2 parts, and make a smooth, oval-shaped loaf from each piece. Place into a lightly oiled bread pan, and let rise for 20 minutes. Preheat the oven to 350°F. Bake for 40 minutes. Cool before slicing.

Per slice: Calories 127, Protein 4 g, Fat 3 g, Carbohydrates 22 g, Fiber 3 g

# *Braided Bread*

### Yield: 8 servings

*This bread is good to pull apart to eat instead of slicing it*

**1 cup lukewarm soymilk**
**½ cup lukewarm water**
**¼ cup liquid sweetener**
**2 teaspoons baking yeast**
**1½ cups unbleached white flour**

**3 tablespoons flaxseeds**
**¾ cup warm water**
**½ teaspoon salt**
**3 tablespoons oil**
**1½ cups whole wheat flour**
**2¾ cups unbleached white flour**

In a medium mixing bowl, combine the soymilk, water, liquid sweetener, baking yeast, and 1½ cups flour. Let rest for 10 minutes to form a sponge.

Process the flaxseeds with the warm water in a blender until the consistency is smooth and creamy and the seeds are broken up into small, dark flecks. Add the flaxseed mixture, salt, oil, and remaining flours to the sponge after it has begun to bubble.

Stir with a wooden spoon, and then turn onto a clean surface to knead. Knead for 5 to 10 minutes. Place the dough into an oiled bowl, and let rise for 30 minutes.

Divide the dough into 3 pieces, and make 20-inch-long ropes out of each piece. Braid them together and gently place the braid on a cookie sheet. Let rise for 20 to 30 minutes. Preheat the oven to 350°F, and bake for 30 to 40 minutes.

Per serving: Calories 396, Protein 11 g, Fat 8 g, Carbohydrates 71 g,
Fiber 6 g

# Sesame-Rice Cornbread

### Yield: 6 to 8 servings

*This is a delicious way to use leftover brown rice and capitalize on the nutritional goodness of these combined grains.*

**3 tablespoons flaxseeds**
**¾ cup warm water**
**1 cup cooked brown rice**
**1 tablespoon molasses**
**1 tablespoon liquid sweetener**
**2 tablespoons sesame oil**
**1 cup soymilk**

*Dry ingredients:*

**1½ cups yellow cornmeal**
**½ cup whole wheat flour**
**1 cup unbleached white flour**
**¼ teaspoon salt**
**3 teaspoons baking powder**

**2 tablespoons sesame seeds**

Preheat the oven to 375°F. Three to 5 minutes before baking, put 1 tablespoon of oil in a 10-inch cast-iron skillet, and place it in the oven to preheat.

Process the flaxseeds with the warm water in a blender until the consistency is smooth and creamy and the seeds are broken up into small, dark flecks. Add the rice, molasses, liquid sweetener, oil, and soymilk, and process until smooth; set aside.

In a medium mixing bowl, combine the dry ingredients. Pour the blender mixture into the dry ingredients, and mix well.

Remove the preheated skillet from the oven, and tilt the pan so the oil spreads evenly. Sprinkle the sesame seeds over the bottom of the skillet. Pour the batter over the sesame seeds, quickly return to the oven, and bake for 25 minutes.

Per serving: Calories 326, Protein 8 g, Fat 7 g, Carbohydrates 56 g, Fiber 6 g

# Orange–Date Muffins

### Yield: 12 muffins

*This has to be one of the tastiest ways to enjoy the tropical flavors of oranges and dates.*

**3 tablespoons flaxseeds**
**1¼ cups orange juice**

**2 tablespoons canola oil**
**3 tablespoons liquid sweetener**
**1½ cups chopped dates**

**1½ cups unbleached white flour**
**1 cup whole wheat flour**
**2 teaspoons baking power**
**1 teaspoon baking soda**
**½ teaspoon salt**

Preheat the oven to 350°F.

Process the flaxseeds and orange juice together in a blender until the consistency is smooth and creamy and the seeds are broken up into small, dark flecks. Pour into a large mixing bowl. Add the oil, liquid sweetener, and dates, and mix all the ingredients together.

Sift the white flour, whole wheat flour, baking powder, baking soda, and salt into the liquid ingredients, and mix well. Pour into lightly oiled muffin tins, and bake for 15 minutes.

The muffins are done when a toothpick inserted in the middle of a muffin comes out clean.

Per muffin: Calories 204, Protein 4 g, Fat 3 g, Carbohydrates 40 g, Fiber 4 g

# *Rhubarb–Raspberry Filled Muffins*

Yield: 12 muffins

*The fruit filling creates a marbled effect in these muffins.*

### *Rhubarb-Raspberry Filling*

1½ cups chopped rhubarb
1 heaping cup fresh or frozen raspberries
½ cup sugar

### *Liquid Ingredients*

1½ tablespoons flaxseeds
½ cup warm water
¾ cup orange juice
½ cup nondairy yogurt
¼ cup liquid sweetener
3 tablespoons canola oil

### *Dry Ingredients*

1 cup unbleached white flour
1 cup whole wheat flour
1½ teaspoons baking powder
1 teaspoon baking soda
¼ teaspoon salt

In a medium saucepan, combine the rhubarb, raspberries, and sugar. Cover and cook for 5 minutes. Remove the lid and cook until a thick jam is formed, about 5 more minutes.

In a blender, whip the liquid ingredients. Pour this creamy liquid into a medium mixing bowl.

Preheat the oven to 350°F.

Sift the dry ingredients into the liquid ingredients, and mix well. Spoon 2 to 3 tablespoons of batter into each lightly oiled muffin tin. They should be only ⅓ full. Spoon 3 tablespoons of the rhubarb-raspberry filling into each partially filled muffin tin. Divide the rest of the batter by spooning it into the muffin tins to cover the berry filling. Fill the muffin tins to the top. Bake for 18 to 20 minutes.

The muffins are done when a toothpick inserted in the middle of a muffin comes out clean.

Per muffin: Calories 173, Protein 3 g, Fat 4 g, Carbohydrates 31 g, Fiber 3 g

# *Very Berry Muffins*

### Yield: 12 muffins

*These muffins are light and full of berries.*

### *Liquid Ingredients*

**1 cup nondairy milk**
**1½ tablespoons flaxseeds**
**½ cup warm water**
**½ cup liquid sweetener**
**3 tablespoons canola oil**
**1 teaspoon vanilla**

### *Dry Ingredients*

**2 cups unbleached white flour**
**½ cup whole wheat flour**
**1½ teaspoons baking powder**
**1 teaspoon baking soda**
**¼ teaspoon salt**

**2 cups berries raspberries, blackberries, strawberries, etc.**
**(fresh or frozen and thawed)**

Preheat the oven to 350°F.

In a blender, process the liquid ingredients until smooth and creamy, and pour into a mixing bowl.

Sift the dry ingredients into the liquid ingredients, and stir until all the dry ingredients are absorbed.

Gently stir the berries into the muffin batter. Spoon into lightly oiled muffin tins, and bake for 20 minutes.

The muffins are done when a toothpick inserted in the middle of a muffin comes out clean.

Per muffin: Calories 179, Protein 3 g, Fat 4 g, Carbohydrates 32 g, Fiber 3 g

# *Wheatless Muffins*

### Yield: 12 muffins

*You won't miss the wheat in these tasty muffins.*

### *Dry Ingredients*

1½ cups barley flour
1 cup oat flour
1 cup cornmeal
3 teaspoons baking powder
½ teaspoon baking soda
½ teaspoon salt
¼ teaspoon cinnamon

1½ tablespoons flaxseeds
½ cup warm water

1⅓ cups soymilk
½ cup liquid sweetener
2 tablespoons canola oil

½ cup raisins
½ cup sunflower seeds

Preheat the oven to 375°F.

Mix the dry ingredients in a medium mixing bowl. Process the flaxseeds with the warm water in a blender until the consistency is smooth and creamy and the seeds are broken up into small, dark flecks.

Add the flaxseed mixture, liquid sweetener, oil, and soymilk to the dry ingredients. Stir well enough to dissolve all the dry ingredients.

Mix in the raisins and sunflower seeds. Spoon into lightly oiled muffin tins, and bake for 18 minutes. The muffins are done when a toothpick inserted in the middle of a muffin comes out clean.

Per muffin: Calories 256, Protein 6 g, Fat 7 g, Carbohydrates 43 g, Fiber 6 g

# *Melina's Herbed*
# *Biscuits*

### Yield: 15 biscuits

*These quick biscuits are flavored with dried herbs that make them a taste treat to accompany any soup. Crumble leftover biscuits up into tossed salad like croutons.*

**1 cup chopped onions and green peppers**
**1 tablespoon water**

### *Dry Ingredients*

**1 cup unbleached white flour**
**1 cup whole wheat flour**
**½ cup cornmeal**
**2 tablespoons nutritional yeast**
**2 tablespoons granulated sweetener**
**½ teaspoon sage**
**½ teaspoon basil**
**½ teaspoon thyme**
**1 tablespoon baking powder**
**½ teaspoon salt**

**½ tablespoon ground flaxseeds**
**3 tablespoons warm water**
**3 tablespoons canola oil**

**¾ cup potato water or water**

Preheat the oven to 375°F.

In a medium skillet, steam-fry the onions and green peppers in the 1 tablespoon water. Stir and cook until soft.

In a medium bowl, mix the dry ingredients.

Process the flaxseeds with the warm water and oil in a blender until the consistency is smooth and creamy and the seeds are broken up into small, dark flecks. Add the flaxseed mixture and cooked onion and pepper to the dry ingredients, and mix well.

Add the potato water to the bowl, and mix until all water has been absorbed. Place the dough on a lightly floured counter, and press out with the palms of your hands. You may need to flour the top of the dough to prevent your hands from sticking.

Roll or press out ½ inch thick, and cut out biscuits using a large biscuit cutter. Place on a cookie sheet, slightly touching, and bake for 15 minutes.

Per muffin: Calories 200, Protein 3 g, Fat 3 g, Carbohydrates 40 g, Fiber 2 g

# *Scones*

### Yield: 12 scones

*Irish raisin biscuits are fun to make and good with soup.*

### *Dry Ingredients*
1½ cups white flour
½ cup whole wheat flour
1½ tablespoons granulated sweetener
2 teaspoons baking powder
½ teaspoon salt

1 tablespoon ground flaxseeds
3 tablespoons warm water
3 tablespoons canola oil

7 tablespoons soy yogurt
½ cup raisins

Preheat the oven to 375°F.

In a medium mixing bowl, combine the dry ingredients.

Process the flaxseeds with the warm water and oil in a blender until the consistency is smooth and creamy and the seeds are broken up into small, dark flecks. Mix the flaxseed mixture into the bowl of dry ingredients. Mix with a fork until well blended.

Add the soy yogurt and raisins, and mix until all the liquid is absorbed. Don't over-mix. Flatten the dough onto a lightly floured counter. With your hands, press the dough out into a ½-inch thick square or rectangle. With a blunt knife, cut into triangles and place on a cookie sheet. Bake for 13 minutes. These are best if served warm.

Per scone: Calories 127, Protein 3 g, Fat 3 g, Carbohydrates 20 g, Fiber 2 g

# Blueberry Bread

**Yield: 10 to 12 slices**

*This works equally well with either fresh or frozen blueberries. Fold in ½ cup chopped walnuts with the blueberries to make a rich dessert bread.*

**¼ cup fresh lemon juice**
**¼ cup canola oil**
**1 cup sugar**
**1 teaspoon vanilla**
**¾ cup soymilk**
**½ cup ground flaxseeds**
**2 cups unbleached white flour**
**2 teaspoons baking powder**
**½ teaspoon baking soda**
**1 cup fresh or frozen/thawed blueberries**

Preheat the oven to 350°F.

In a medium mixing bowl, stir the lemon juice, oil, sugar, vanilla, and soymilk with a whisk. Add the flaxseeds. Sift in the flour, baking powder, and soda. Stir well and add the blueberries. Mix gently with only a few strokes. Pour the batter into a lightly oiled bread pan Bake for 45 to 55 minutes. It will take longer to bake if your blueberries are not fresh.

Let cool before slicing.

Per slice: Calories 219, Protein 4 g, Fat 8 g, Carbohydrates 36 g, Fiber 2 g

# *Escatcha*

### Yield: 10 servings

*This wonderful Sicilian stuffed bread is good hot or cold. It's the perfect thing to take on a picnic.*

### *Dough*

2 cups unbleached white flour
2 cups whole wheat flour
½ cup ground flaxseeds
½ teaspoon salt
1⅓ tablespoons baking powder
3 tablespoons canola oil (plus a little to spread over the top before baking)
1½ cups soymilk

### *Filling*

1 cup chopped onions
1 teaspoon olive oil
4 ounces fresh or canned mushrooms, sliced
1 pound frozen spinach, cooked
1 pound firm tofu, crumbled
¼ cup nutritional yeast (optional)
⅛ teaspoon black pepper
1 teaspoon garlic powder
1 teaspoon oregano
1 teaspoon basil
2 tablespoons soy sauce
1 tablespoon balsamic vinegar

Preheat the oven to 375°F.

Combine the dough ingredients in a mixing bowl. You can use your hands to mix it after initially stirring it with a wooden spoon. Form it into a ball, and set it aside until the filling is ready.

In a large skillet, sauté the onions and mushrooms (if using fresh) in the olive oil until browned. If using canned mushrooms, add with the spinach and heat until all the liquid has cooked out. Add the crumbled tofu, nutritional yeast, pepper, garlic, oregano, basil, soy sauce, and vinegar. Stir well and cook until heated. Turn off the heat and cover while you prepare the dough.

Roll the dough out on a lightly oiled surface into a large oval so the dough is just less than ½ inch thick. Gently move the dough to a large cookie sheet. Spread the filling evenly over half of the dough. Pull the remaining dough up and over the filling, and pinch the edges together. Spread a little olive oil over the top of the crust. Bake for 45 minutes. Slice and serve.

Per serving: Calories 295, Protein 12 g, Fat 11 g, Carbohydrates 41 g, Fiber 7 g

# *Banana Bread*

### Yield: 8 to 10 slices

*Both flax oil and flaxseeds combine here in this delicious dessert bread.*

### Liquid ingredients

3 bananas, mashed
2 tablespoons flax oil
½ cup honey
1 teaspoon vanilla
3 tablespoons soy yogurt or soymilk

### Dry ingredients

1½ cups unbleached white flour
1 cup whole wheat pastry flour
1 teaspoon baking soda
1 teaspoon baking powder
½ teaspoon salt

¼ cup ground flaxseeds

Preheat the oven to 350°F.

In a medium mixing bowl, stir together the liquid ingredients. Sift the dry ingredients into the liquid ingredients. Add the flaxseeds and stir well.

Bake for 45 minutes. The bread is done when a toothpick inserted in the middle comes out clean. Let cool before slicing.

Per serving: Calories 246, Protein 5 g, Fat 5 g, Carbohydrates 46 g, Fiber 4 g

# Flax-The Super Food

# Spreads and Dips

# *Mushroom–Walnut Pâté*

### Yield: 2⅓ cups

*A mild, crunchy spread for crackers, raw vegetables, or bagels.*

**1½ cups chopped onions**
**1 teaspoon olive oil**
**3 cups sliced fresh mushrooms**
**1 cup walnuts**
**2 tablespoons sweet barley miso**
**¼ cup nutritional yeast**
**¼ cup ground flaxseeds**
**One 12.3-ounce box firm silken tofu**

Cook the onions in the oil until browned. Add the mushrooms, cover, and cook, stirring occasionally, until the water has exuded from the mushrooms. Toast the walnuts in a dry skillet while stirring.

Pour the onion-mushroom mixture and walnuts into a food processor along with the miso, nutritional yeast, flaxseeds, and tofu. Process for a short while until well blended but not smooth.

Per 2 tablespoons: Calories 77, Protein 3 g, Fat 5 g, Carbohydrates 5 g, Fiber 1 g

# *White Bean Pâté*

Yield: 2½ cups

*This versatile pâté can be served warm or cold. For an interesting appetizer, try spreading this on warmed tortillas, roll up, and cut into 1-inch sections to make pinwheels.*

**2 cups cooked white beans (such as navy or lima), mashed**
**⅓ cup finely chopped tomatoes**
**¼ cup minced red onions**
**2 tablespoons flax oil**
**½ teaspoon cumin**
**¼ teaspoon salt**
**⅛ teaspoon black pepper**
**Juice of 1 lemon**

Drain and mash the cooked beans.

While the beans are hot, add the rest of the ingredients, and mix well. Serve while warm or chill until cold.

Per 2 tablespoons: Calories 35, Protein 1 g, Fat 1 g, Carbohydrates 4 g, Fiber 1 g

# Guacamole Olé

*Make traditional guacamole even more nutritious by adding these fresh veggies. To make a spicier version, try adding ½ teaspoon chopped jalapeños.*

**Yield: approximately 3 cups (6 servings)**

**2 large, ripe avocados**
**½ cup plain soy yogurt**
**2 to 3 tablespoons freshly squeezed lime juice**
**2 teaspoons flax oil**
**2 teaspoons olive oil**
**½ teaspoon sea salt**
**½ teaspoon garlic granules**
**¼ cup diced yellow bell pepper**
**¼ cup diced red bell pepper**
**2 tablespoons diced red onion**

Peel and mash the avocados with a fork in a medium-sized bowl.

Add the yogurt, lime juice, flax and olive oil, and seasonings, and stir well.

Fold in the chopped peppers and onion.

Chill and serve in a scooped out red, green, or yellow bell pepper or acorn squash. This is great served with Baked Pita Chips (see recipe below), stuffed in pita bread with grated carrots and sprouts, or added to burritos or tacos.

Per serving: Calories 151, Protein 2 g, Fat 11 g, Carbohydrates 10 g, Fiber 3 g

### *Baked Pita Chips*

**3 whole wheat pita breads**

Preheat the oven to 300°F.

Cut the pita bread in half crosswise. Pull the halves apart, stack them, and cut in half. Cut each half into three wedges.

Place the wedges on an ungreased cookie sheet, and bake for 30 minutes until browned and crisp. Be sure to turn the wedges occasionally.

# *Hummus*

**Yield: 2 cups**

*This rich spread is the natural accompaniment to pita bread topped with sprouts and tomato. It also makes a great travel food to put in your cooler and eat with crackers or chips.*

**2 cups cooked garbanzo beans**
**¼ cup lemon juice**
**2 cloves garlic**
**2 tablespoons tahini**
**2 tablespoons bean stock**
**2 tablespoons flax oil**
**½ cup chopped fresh parsley**
**1 tablespoon soy sauce**

Purée all of the ingredients together. Let them rest for a least 30 minutes before serving to let the flavors develop.

Per ¼ cup: Calories 123, Protein 4 g, Fat 6 g, Carbohydrates 13 g, Fiber 3 g

# *Artichoke Heart Dip*

### Yield: 3¾ cups

*This is a thick dip or spread that you can enjoy on bagels, with baked potatoes (sweet and white), with raw carrot sticks, or over steamed vegetables.*

**3 tablespoons fresh lemon juice**
**2 cups crumbled firm tofu**
**One 13¾-ounce jar quartered artichoke hearts,**
    **packed in water**
**2 large cloves garlic, chopped**
**2 tablespoons soy sauce**
**4 tablespoons nutritional yeast**
**2 tablespoons flax oil**
**2 tablespoons soy mayonnaise**

Blend all the ingredients in a food processor until smooth. This will not be creamy because the artichoke hearts give it some texture.

Per 2 tablespoons: Calories 33, Protein 2 g, Fat 2 g, Carbohydrates 2 g, Fiber 0 g

# *West Indies Bean Dip*

Yield: 2⅔ cups

*Here is a spicy dip that is good to serve with corn chips as an appetizer or party snack.*

2½ cups cooked pinto or kidney beans
¼ cup finely chopped onions
1 tomato, chopped (about ⅔ cup)
3 tablespoons flax oil
2 tablespoons lemon or lime juice
1 tablespoon soy sauce
1 teaspoon coriander
1 teaspoon cumin
½ teaspoon curry powder
½ teaspoon oregano
½ teaspoon chili powder
2 cloves garlic, minced

Blend all of the ingredients together in a food processor, or mash the beans with a fork and mix well with all of the other ingredients.

Per 2 tablespoons: Calories 48, Protein 2 g, Fat 2 g, Carbohydrates 6 g, Fiber 1 g

# *Savory Cream Cheese Ball*

### Yield: 3 cups

*This is a quick and delicious recipe to whip up for a party.*

**Two 8-ounce packages soy cream cheese, softened**
**2 carrots, peeled and grated (about 1½ cups)**
**4 scallions, chopped**
**1 teaspoon flax oil**
**1 teaspoon vegetarian Worcestershire sauce**

Combine all the ingredients in a bowl. Cover and refrigerate for at least 2 hours.

Shape the cheese mixture into a ball, and place on a large serving plate.

Per 2 tablespoons: Calories 32, Protein 1 g, Fat 2 g, Carbohydrates 3 g, Fiber 0 g

### Mr. Clown Cream Cheese Ball

*Here is something fun to make for a children's party that
your kids can help you decorate.*

**1 recipe Savory Cream Cheese Ball, facing page**
**1½ cups grated carrots**
**1 pita bread or 10-inch tortilla**
**1 cherry tomato**
**1 slice of tomato or apple**
**2 carrot or radish rounds**
**2 raisins or olive rounds**
**14 slices soy bologna (optional)**
**Approximately 21 red grapes (optional)**
**Puffed cheese snacks**

Make the Savory Cream Cheese Ball on the facing page. Sprinkle the
grated carrots on the top for hair.

Cut a piece of pita bread into a large triangle for a hat, or roll a 10-
inch flour tortilla into a cone for a hat, and place on top of the head.

Decorate the face with a cherry tomato for a nose, a tomato or apple
slice for a mouth, 2 radish or carrot rounds for the eyes, and round
slices of olives or raisins for the pupils. To form a ruffled collar, fold
soy bologna slices in half, then fold again into quarters. Tuck the
corners of the slices under the mixture and, if desired, fill the open-
ings with red grapes.

Surround the head with puffed cheese snacks. Serve with fresh vegetables such as carrots, red peppers, celery, etc., and your favorite
crackers.

Per 2 tablespoons: Calories 41, Protein 1 g, Fat 2 g, Carbohydrates 5 g,
Fiber 1 g

# *Fresh Salsa*

### Yield: 2 cups

*Fresh homemade salsa is reason enough to have cilantro growing outside your house.*

**8 Roma tomatoes, cored, chopped, and drained**
**(about 2 pounds)**
**¼ cup chopped red onion**
**1 clove garlic, minced**
**1 teaspoon chopped jalapeño pepper**
**2 tablespoons freshly squeezed lime juice**
**2 tablespoons chopped fresh cilantro or parsley**
**1 tablespoon olive oil**
**2 to 3 teaspoons flax oil**
**¼ teaspoon sea salt**

Combine the chopped tomatoes with all the remaining ingredients. This can be eaten immediately but is best if allowed to chill for about 2 hours so the flavors can blend. Serve with baked pita chips or your favorite corn chips.

*Vegetarian Tacos: Fill taco shells with vegetarian refried beans, and bake at 350°F for 15 minutes until crispy. Serve with chopped tomatoes, chopped yellow onions, shredded lettuce, guacamole, and top with this yummy salsa.*

Per 2 tablespoons: Calories 26, Protein 0 g, Fat 2 g, Carbohydrates 3 g, Fiber 1 g

# Flax–The Super Food

# Salads and Dressings

# *Zesty Green Bean Salad*

Yield: 6 servings

*A tangy dressing brings this combination of beans alive.*

**3 cups green beans, cut diagonally**

**2 cups cooked white beans or lima beans**

**2 cloves garlic, minced**
**½ cup lime juice**
**3 tablespoons soy sauce**
**2 tablespoons flax oil or chili-garlic flax oil**
**1 tablespoon sugar**
**¼ teaspoon salt**
**1 fresh chile or jalapeño pepper, seeded and thinly chopped**
**   (optional)**
**½ cup minced fresh mint leaves**

Cook the green beans until crisp-tender. Cool with cold water.

Cook the white beans until they are soft but not mushy.

To prepare the dressing, combine the garlic, lime juice, soy sauce, flax oil, sugar, salt, pepper, and mint in a jar with a tightly fitting lid, and shake vigorously until well mixed.

Combine the green beans and white beans in a serving bowl, and pour the dressing over the beans, mixing carefully so the beans stay whole. Refrigerate at least an hour before serving.

Per serving: Calories 145, Protein 6 g, Fat 5 g, Carbohydrates 20 g, Fiber 4 g

# *Pasta Bean Salad*

### Yield: 6 servings

*The addition of pinto beans makes this pasta salad a meal in a bowl.*

**2 cups broccoli, chopped into bite-sized spears**
**½ cup carrots, cut into matchsticks**
**1½ cups cooked small shell pasta, spirals, or elbows**
**½ cup sliced scallions**
**1 bell pepper, chopped**
**2 cups cooked pinto beans, chilled**
**¼ cup chopped fresh parsley**

### *Dressing*

**¼ cup lemon juice**
**2 cloves garlic, minced**
**2 tablespoons soy sauce**
**3 tablespoons flax oil**
**1 teaspoon crushed basil**

Blanch the broccoli and carrots for 3 minutes; drain, rinse with cold water, and set aside.

Combine the pasta, broccoli, carrots, scallions, bell pepper, pinto beans, and parsley in a salad bowl.

To prepare the dressing, combine the lemon juice, garlic, soy sauce, flax oil, and basil in a blender, or place in a jar with a tightly fitting lid, and shake vigorously until well mixed. Toss the salad with the dressing, and serve.

Per serving: Calories 200, Protein 6 g, Fat 7 g, Carbohydrates 27 g, Fiber 5 g

# *Carrot and Garbanzo Salad*

### Yield: 4 to 6 servings

*Prepare this salad ahead of time, and let it marinate for the full flavor to develop.*

**One 15-ounce can garbanzo beans
    (2 cups cooked)**
**1 cup grated carrots**
**1 cup grated cucumbers**
**1 clove garlic, pressed**
**2 scallions, finely chopped**
**¼ cup minced fresh parsley**

### *Dressing*
**2 tablespoons tahini**
**2 tablespoons flax oil**
**2 tablespoons balsamic vinegar**
**1 teaspoon soy sauce**

Combine the beans, carrots, cucumbers, garlic, scallions, and parsley in a medium serving bowl.

Combine the dressing ingredients in a small jar with a tightly fitting lid, and shake vigorously until well blended. Pour the dressing over the salad, mix, and refrigerate a few hours before serving. Stir the salad a few times while it is in the refrigerator.

Per serving: Calories 210, Protein 6 g, Fat 9 g, Carbohydrates 24 g, Fiber 6 g

# *Mock Tuna Salad*

### Yield: 3½ cups

*You don't have to miss the comfort of tuna-style sandwiches any longer. Enjoy this spread with a chunk of Italian or dark rye bread.*

**1 clove garlic, chopped**
**¼ cup chopped onions**
**2 stalks celery, chopped**
**½ cup chopped fresh parsley**
**⅓ cup soy mayonnaise**
**1 tablespoon chopped fresh basil,**
**    or 1 teaspoon dried basil**
**1 teaspoon chopped fresh oregano,**
**    or ½ teaspoon dried oregano**
**¼ teaspoon cumin**
**3 cups cooked garbanzo beans, chopped**
**¼ cup bean stock**
**3 tablespoons flax oil**
**2 tablespoons fresh lemon juice**
**½ teaspoon salt**

Mix all of the ingredients together with a fork, and serve chilled.

Per ⅓ cup: Calories 138, Protein 4 g, Fat 6 g, Carbohydrates 15 g, Fiber 3 g

# *Tropical Black Bean Salad*

### Yield: 6 servings

*This unusual combination of ingredients makes a unique salad or entree. Serve it with fresh corn bread or a loaf of dark pumpernickel.*

**3 cups cooked black beans, cooled**
**2 to 3 mangoes, cubed (2 cups)**
**2 cups chopped fresh pineapple**
**½ cup chopped onions**
**3 cloves garlic, minced**
**1 jalapeño pepper, minced**
**3 tablespoons fresh lime juice**
**2 tablespoons flax oil**
**½ teaspoon salt**

In a medium serving bowl, combine all of the ingredients, stir gently, and serve. You can also refrigerate this salad overnight before serving.

Per serving: Calories 221, Protein 7 g, Fat 5 g, Carbohydrates 36 g, Fiber 6 g

# Marinated Cucumbers

### Yield: 4 servings

*For a variation, use raspberry vinegar instead of the brown rice vinegar*

**2 teaspoons flax oil**
**3 teaspoons brown rice vinegar**
**2 cucumbers, peeled, seeds removed, and chopped**

Mix together the dressing and the cucumbers, and let marinate for at least an hour.

Per serving: Calories 40, Protein 1 g, Fat 2 g, Carbohydrates 4 g, Fiber 2 g

# *Sweet Bulgur Salad*

### Yield: 6 servings

*This is a variation on Middle Eastern tabbouleh, which tra-
ditionally contains mostly parsley and a small amount of
bulgur. Americans tend to like their tabbouleh with a lot
more bulgur. Adding red pepper adds to the vitamin content
of the salad.*

**1 cup bulgur**
**1 cup boiling water**
**1 cup packed chopped Italian flat parsley**
**1 cup minced fresh mint (optional)**
**½ cup chopped red bell pepper**
**4 scallions, chopped**
**2 tablespoons flax oil**
**¼ cup lemon juice**
**½ cup orange juice**
**2 tablespoons soy sauce**
**½ teaspoon sea salt**
**1 teaspoon cumin**
**1 teaspoon basil**

Dry roast the bulgur in a small skillet over medium heat for 5 minutes until a nutty aroma is emitted, stirring occasionally. Rinse the
bulgur and drain.

Place the bulgur in a medium bowl, and cover with 1 cup boiling
water. Let sit approximately 1 hour until the liquid is absorbed. Turn
out into a colander and press somewhat dry, then add the chopped
vegetables.

In a small bowl, make a dressing by mixing together the flax oil,
lemon juice, orange juice, soy sauce, sea salt, cumin, and basil. Pour
over the bulgur and vegetables, and mix together. Refrigerate until
time to serve.

Per serving: Calories 175, Protein 5 g, Fat 5 g, Carbohydrates 28 g, Fiber 4 g

# *Spinach Salad with Miso Dressing*

### Yield: 6 to 8 servings

*Peas add a hint of sweetness to this classic salad.*

**1 pound spinach, stems discarded**
**1 small head Romaine lettuce**
**1 small red onion**
**4 ounces button mushrooms, wiped clean
    and thinly sliced**
**½ cup frozen green peas, thawed**

*Miso Dressing*
  **¼ cup flax oil**
  **¼ cup water**
  **2 tablespoons brown rice syrup
    or other liquid sweetener**
  **2 tablespoons soy sauce**
  **2 tablespoons fresh lemon juice**
  **2 tablespoons barley miso**
  **1 large clove garlic, minced**
  **3 scallions, chopped**
  **Dash of cayenne**

Wash the spinach and Romaine lettuce well, taking care to rinse the underside of the leaves. Dry and tear the leaves into a medium salad bowl. Add the red onion, mushrooms, and green peas.

To make the miso dressing, combine the flax oil, water, brown rice syrup, soy sauce, miso, garlic, scallions, and cayenne in a blender.

Toss gently with the salad, and serve at once. Garnish with croutons, if desired.

*Variation: Use the Garlic Herb Dressing (page 70) instead of the Miso Dressing.*

Per serving: Calories 138, Protein 3 g, Fat 8 g, Carbohydrates 13 g, Fiber 4 g

# *Broccoli and Red Potato Salad*

**Yield: 8 servings**

*This presentation is a departure from traditional warm potato salads.*

**5 red skin potatoes**
**1 pound broccoli**
**2 tablespoons flax oil**
**2 tablespoons olive oil**
**3 tablespoons red wine vinegar**
**3 tablespoons orange juice**
**3 tablespoons minced fresh parsley**
**2 cloves garlic, minced**
**¼ to ½ teaspoon sea salt**
**3 scallions, sliced with the tops**
**One 4-ounce jar pimientos, drained**
**¼ teaspoon cayenne**
**Umeboshi plum vinegar, to taste**

Clean the potatoes, leaving the skins on, and chop into chunks. Boil in a medium pot for about 10 to 15 minutes until tender. Drain and cover to keep warm.

Peel and chop the broccoli stems, and break apart the flowers on the broccoli. Steam the broccoli stems and pieces for about 5 minutes until tender. Set aside and keep covered to stay warm.

In a small mixing bowl, mix together the oils and vinegar along with the parsley, garlic, salt, scallions, pimentos, and cayenne.

Arrange the potatoes in the middle of a serving platter with the broccoli all around the edges, and pour the dressing over them. Sprinkle some umeboshi vinegar over the top, to taste. (Be careful—umeboshi is very strong and salty, so use sparingly.)

Garnish with cherry tomatoes and/or parsley or fresh basil leaves.

Per serving: Calories 152, Protein 2 g, Fat 6 g, Carbohydrates 21 g, Fiber 4 g

# *Broccoli Slaw*

### Yield: 6½ cups

*This is the perfect combination to fill any roll-up style sandwich, be it a tortilla, pita, or chapati.*

**1 head broccoli (approximately 1½ pounds)**
**1 head cauliflower**
**1 cup shredded soy cheddar cheese**
**¾ cup soy mayonnaise**
**1¼ teaspoons flax oil**
**1 tablespoon soymilk**
**1 tablespoon water**
**1 tablespoon maple syrup**
**2 tablespoons soy bacon bits (optional)**

Finely chop the broccoli flowers. Peel the stems and chop up finely. Finely chop the cauliflower and some of its stems. Add together in a large mixing bowl.

Add the soy cheddar cheese to the vegetable mixture, and stir gently.

To make a dressing, mix together the mayonnaise, flax oil, soymilk, water, and maple syrup in a small mixing bowl. Add the dressing to the vegetable mixture, and mix until well blended. Chill. Top with soy bacon bits, if desired, and serve.

Per ½ cup: Calories 81, Protein 3 g, Fat 4 g, Carbohydrates 6 g, Fiber 3 g

# *Tofu Salad*

### Yield: 3⅓ cups

*Don't stop with tofu salad sandwiches—try this stuffed in fresh tomatoes.*

**1½ tablespoons toasted sesame seeds**
**1 cup chopped celery**
**½ cup minced onion**
**¼ cup nutritional yeast**
**1½ teaspoons dried dill**
**½ teaspoon garlic granules**
**3 cups mashed firm tofu**
**½ cup chopped fresh parsley**
**2 tablespoons rice vinegar**
**2 tablespoons flax oil**
**1 tablespoon spicy mustard**
**2 tablespoons soy sauce**
**Salt and pepper, to taste**

In a medium mixing bowl, add the sesame seeds, celery, onion, nutritional yeast, dill, garlic, and 2 cups of the mashed tofu.

In a food processor, blend together the remaining 1 cup of mashed tofu with the parsley, rice vinegar, flax oil, mustard, and soy sauce. Add this puréed mixture to the mixing bowl, and stir until everything is well blended. Add salt and pepper to taste.

Per ⅓ cup: Calories 109, Protein 7 g, Fat 7 g, Carbohydrates 5 g, Fiber 1 g

# *Mother Earth's Herb Dressing*

### Yield: 2 cups

*This delicious basic dressing will become a favorite you'll want to have on hand for all your salad greens.*

**1 cup olive oil**
**½ cup flax oil**
**5 tablespoons brown rice vinegar**
**3 to 4 cloves garlic, finely chopped**
**4 tablespoons finely chopped fresh basil**
**¼ teaspoon Spike seasoning**
**1 teaspoon lemon juice**
**Dash of soy sauce**
**Tarragon, parsley, and rosemary, to taste**

Mix all the above ingredients together in a blender. Keep stored in the refrigerator.

Per tablespoon: Calories 90, Protein 0 g, Fat 10 g, Carbohydrates 0 g, Fiber 0 g

# *Garlic Herb Dressing*

Yield: 1 cup

*Serve this tangy dressing on spinach salad and steamed vegetables such as broccoli and kale. Mirin is rice wine vinegar, which can be used here instead of white wine.*

¼ **cup flax oil**
¼ **cup olive oil**
¼ **cup plus 1 tablespoon soy sauce**
**3 tablespoons red wine vinegar**
**1 tablespoon mirin, white wine, or sherry**
¼ **cup unsweetened ketchup**
**1 teaspoon lemon juice**
¾ **teaspoon vegetarian Worcestershire sauce**
**1 tablespoon crushed garlic**
**1 teaspoon mixed Italian herbs**
**1 teaspoon maple syrup**

Combine all the ingredients together in a blender or a jar with a tightly fitting lid. For a thinner dressing, add more mirin. For a slightly spicier flavor, add a dash or two of hot sauce.

Per tablespoon: Calories 68, Protein 1 g, Fat 6 g, Carbohydrates 2 g, Fiber 0 g

# *Spicy Peanut Dressing*

### Yield 1¼ cups

*The inspiration for this dressing comes from Thai cuisine, which is quickly becoming a favorite with gourmets everywhere. It makes a delicious topping for any type of food, including hot or cold pasta and steamed vegetables.*

**½ cup natural peanut butter**
**2 tablespoons flax oil**
**2 tablespoons water**
**3 tablespoons soy sauce**
**3 tablespoons brown rice vinegar**
**3 tablespoons brown sugar**
**1 teaspoon chili powder**

Combine all the ingredients in a blender until smooth.

Per tablespoon: Calories 57, Protein 2 g, Fat 3 g, Carbohydrates 3 g, Fiber 1 g

# Tahini Miso Dressing

### Yield: 1 cup

*As simple as this dressing is to prepare, the flavors are complex and inviting. It makes a rich and hearty topping for steamed vegetables as well as salad greens.*

**1 clove garlic**
**3 tablespoons rice vinegar**
**2 tablespoons barley miso**
**2 tablespoons soy sauce**
**2 tablespoons tahini**
**2 tablespoons flax oil**

Combine all the ingredients in a blender until smooth. Add a little water if it seems too thick.

Per tablespoon: Calories 32, Protein 1 g, Fat 2 g, Carbohydrates 1 g, Fiber 0 g

# Green Goddess Dressing

### Yield: ¾ cup

*Now you can make this favorite dressing at home and enjoy the benefits of flax oil as well.*

**1 avocado**
**2 cloves garlic**
**¼ cup lemon juice**
**2 tablespoons flax oil**
**¼ cup chopped fresh parsley**
**¼ cup soy mayonnaise**

Combine all the ingredients in a blender. Serve over tossed salad or steamed vegetables.

Per tablespoon: Calories 62, Protein 0 g, Fat 5 g, Carbohydrates 3 g, Fiber 1 g

# Orange Sesame Dressing

**Yield: 1¼ cups**

*This dressing is a light, fresh topping for mesclun greens. For an unusual twist, try it over baked sweet potatoes. If you don't have toasted sesame seeds, roast them lightly in a dry skillet until just starting to brown.*

**2 tablespoons toasted sesame seeds**
**3 cloves garlic, minced**
**¼ cup flax oil**
**1 tablespoon tamari**
**⅔ cup fresh orange juice**
**1 tablespoon rice vinegar**

Place all the ingredients in a blender, and process until smooth.

Per tablespoon: Calories 34, Protein 0 g, Fat 3 g, Carbohydrates 1 g, Fiber 0 g

# *Sweet and Sour Sauce*

### Yield 1¼ cups

*This is the perennial favorite for stir-frys and spring rolls. Also try it uncooked as a marinade for tofu, seitan, or textured soy chunks before grilling.*

**1 cup pineapple juice**
**2 tablespoons cornstarch**
**3 tablespoons brown sugar**
**2 tablespoons apple cider vinegar**
**1 tablespoon soy sauce**
**1 tablespoon flax oil**

In a medium saucepan, combine the pineapple juice, cornstarch, brown sugar, apple cider vinegar, and soy sauce over medium heat. Stir constantly until the sauce thickens, and cook gently for 1 minute. Remove from the heat and add the flax oil. Beat until smooth and creamy.

Per tablespoon: Calories 44, Protein 0 g, Fat 1 g, Carbohydrates 8 g, Fiber 0 g

# Flax–The Super Food

# Soups

# *Spicy Split Pea Soup*

**Yield: 4 servings**

*Be ready for an exotic treat when you embellish the plain split pea with this array of spices. Or, if you prefer, use just the spices you like or have on hand.*

**1½ cups dry split peas
5 cups water
1½ cups chopped onions
1 cup chopped tomatoes
1 chili pepper, minced
½ teaspoon ginger powder
½ teaspoon garlic granules
½ teaspoon cardamom
1 teaspoon turmeric
2 teaspoons coriander
2 teaspoons cumin
½ teaspoon chili powder**

**2 tablespoons ground flaxseeds**

In a heavy soup pot, combine all of the ingredients, except the flaxseeds, and bring to a boil. Lower to a simmer, and cook, partially covered, for 1½ hours. The split peas should become soft and begin to disintegrate. Add salt to taste after the soup has cooked. Top each serving with the ground flaxseeds.

Per serving: Calories 277, Protein 16 g, Fat 2 g, Carbohydrates 49 g, Fiber 13 g

# Black Bean Soup

**Yield: 6 servings**

*Eating black beans, dark and warming, is comforting any time of the year. With or without the scoop of rice, cornmeal muffins go well with this soup.*

**2 cups dry black beans (1 pound)**
**8 cups water**
**1 bay leaf**
**1 large onion, finely chopped**
**1 green bell pepper, chopped**

**1 teaspoon oregano**
**2 teaspoons cumin**
**1 teaspoon salt**
**2 tablespoons lemon juice**

**2 tablespoons flax oil**

**3 cups cooked rice (optional)**
**Chopped scallions, for garnish**

Soak the beans overnight in enough water to cover; drain and rinse. In a soup pot, combine the soaked beans with the water, bay leaf, onion, and green pepper, and simmer for 1½ to 2 hours until the beans are very soft.

Add the oregano, cumin, salt, and lemon juice, and cook for 5 more minutes. Stir in the flax oil. Serve with a scoop of cooked rice in the middle of each bowl, if you wish, and garnish with chopped scallions.

Per serving: Calories 242, Protein 11 g, Fat 5 g, Carbohydrates 37 g, Fiber 8 g

# *Lentil Soup with Greens*

### Yield: 6 servings

*This soup is like a hearty stew. Enjoy it with a chunk of corn bread or crusty Italian bread.*

**1½ cups dry lentils**
**8 cups water**

**1 cup chopped onions**
**3 cloves garlic, minced**
**1 teaspoon canola oil**

**6 cups chopped greens (spinach, Swiss chard, collards, kale, etc.)**
**¼ cup chopped parsley**
**2 tablespoons tomato paste**
**½ teaspoon cumin powder**
**½ teaspoon crushed chili peppers**
**½ teaspoon salt**

**2 tablespoons ground flaxseeds**

Rinse the lentils well, then bring to a boil in the water. Lower the heat to a simmer, and cook gently for 45 minutes.

Sauté the onions and garlic in the canola oil for 5 minutes. Add to the lentils along with the chopped greens, parsley, tomato paste, and spices, and stir well. Cook over medium heat for 15 minutes. Serve topped with the ground flaxseeds.

Per serving: Calories 219, Protein 13 g, Fat 2 g, Carbohydrates 37 g, Fiber 9 g

# *Creamy Corn Soup*

**Yield: 5 to 6 servings**

*Kids love this creamy soup with corn and a dash of dill.*

**3 cups cooked lima beans**
**3 cups bean stock or vegetable broth**

**¾ cup chopped onions**
**1 teaspoon canola oil**
**2 cups fresh or frozen corn**

**2 tablespoons flour**
**2 tablespoons chopped fresh dill,**
    **or 1 teaspoon dried dill**
**½ teaspoon salt**
**⅛ teaspoon black pepper**

**1½ cups soymilk**
**2 tablespoons flax oil**

Blend the beans and broth in a food processor or in batches in a blender, and set aside.

In a medium soup pot, sauté the onions in the canola oil until soft, add the corn, and cook until hot.

Stir the flour, dill, salt, and black pepper into the pot with the onions and corn.

Gradually add the soymilk and stir until any lumps dissolve. Simmer for 3 minutes, add the bean purée, and heat slowly until hot throughout. Stir in the flax oil, and serve immediately.

Per serving: Calories 263, Protein 10 g, Fat 7 g, Carbohydrates 39 g, Fiber 10 g

# *Asparagus Soup*

### Yield: 10 cups

*Be sure to use fresh asparagus so you can enjoy its subtle flavor.*

**6 cups stock or water**
**2 pounds asparagus, chopped**
   **(Set the tips aside to add later.)**
**3 cups chopped potatoes**
**1½ cups chopped celery**
**1 large onion**

**The asparagus tips**
**1 teaspoon dried basil**
**1 teaspoon salt**
**⅛ teaspoon black pepper**

**1¾ cups nondairy milk**
**2 tablespoons ground flaxseeds**

Place the stock or water, asparagus, potatoes, celery, and onion in a soup pot. Bring to a boil and simmer until everything is soft, about 10 minutes. Blend the soup in a food processor in several small batches, and return to the pot.

Add the asparagus tips, basil, salt, and black pepper to the blended soup, and simmer for 5 minutes.

Add the milk and flaxseeds, stir well, and turn off the heat. Do not boil the soup after adding the milk, it may separate.

Per serving: Calories 183, Protein 7 g, Fat 3 g, Carbohydrates 32 g, Fiber 8 g

# Flax-The Super Food

# Entrees

# *Enchiladas*

### Yield: 6 to 8 servings

*This is an easy dish to prepare, especially if your beans are already cooked. We like it on cool fall evenings, accompanied by a fresh green salad.*

### *Filling*

1 cup chopped onions
3 cloves garlic, minced
½ teaspoon canola oil
4 cups cooked pinto beans
½ cup bean stock or vegetable broth
1 tablespoon tomato paste
2 tablespoons soy sauce
1 teaspoon cumin

### *Sauce*

½ cup chopped onions
½ cup chopped green bell peppers
1 tablespoon minced garlic
½ teaspoon canola oil
3 cups puréed tomatoes
2 cups water
3 ½ tablespoons chili powder
2 teaspoons cumin
½ teaspoon oregano
3 tablespoons ground flaxseeds

In a heavy skillet, sauté the 1 cup onions and 3 cloves garlic in the ½ teaspoon canola oil until the onions are soft.

Add the beans, bean stock, tomato paste, soy sauce, and cumin to the skillet, and simmer for 8 to 10 minutes. Turn off the heat and mash the beans.

While the bean filling is cooking, make the sauce by sautéing the ½ cup onions, green peppers, and 1 tablespoon garlic in the remaining ½ teaspoon canola oil in a heavy, 2-quart saucepan. Add the tomatoes, water, and spices, and simmer for 10 minutes, stirring occasionally to prevent sticking. Turn off the heat and stir in the ground flaxseeds.

Preheat the oven to 350°F, and lightly oil a 9 x 13-inch baking dish. Scoop 1 cup of the sauce into the baking dish, and spread it around to cover the bottom. Take a tortilla with a pair of tongs, and dip it into the tomato sauce. (This keeps the tortilla from cracking when it is folded over). Place it on an empty plate to assemble. Spoon ⅓ cup of the filling along the center of the tortilla, and wrap it around the bean filling. Place it in the baking dish with the overlap side down. When all of the tortillas are rolled and in the pan, pour the remaining sauce over the top, and bake for 20 to 25 minutes.

Per serving: Calories 214, Protein 9 g, Fat 3 g, Carbohydrates 39 g, Fiber 8 g

# Tamale-Stuffed Peppers

### Yield: 6 servings

*Take stuffed peppers to a new level with this Southwestern take on the traditional favorite.*

**6 green or red bell peppers**

**1 cup chopped onions**
**3 cloves garlic, minced**
**1 teaspoon canola oil**

**3 cups chopped tomatoes**
**¾ cup cornmeal**
**1½ tablespoons chili powder**
**1½ teaspoons cumin**
**½ teaspoon salt**

**2 cups cooked black beans**
**1½ cups frozen corn**
**3 tablespoons ground flaxseeds**

Slice the tops off the peppers, and remove the seeds. Blanch them in 1 inch of boiling water for 5 minutes. Drain and set aside while you prepare the filling.

In a medium skillet, sauté the onions and garlic in the canola oil until soft.

Add the tomatoes, cornmeal, chili powder, cumin, and salt to the sautéed onions and garlic, and cook until thick, stirring constantly. Turn off the heat and stir in the ground flaxseeds.

Preheat the oven to 350°F.

Add the black beans and corn to the skillet, and cook until hot. Fill each steamed pepper with ⅙ of the filling. Put them upright in a shallow baking dish, pour ½ inch of water into the baking dish, and bake for 25 minutes.

Per serving: Calories 239, Protein 8 g, Fat 4 g, Carbohydrates 45 g,
Fiber 10 g

# *Falafel*

### Yield: twenty 1-inch balls

*These balls can be served in pita bread with fresh vegetables, soy yogurt, and tahini sauce as toppings. These falafel are baked instead of fried and which makes them lower in fat than traditional falafel. If you have any leftovers, they can be flattened and used in sandwiches.*

**3 cups cooked garbanzo beans**
**1 small onion, finely chopped**
**¼ teaspoon garlic granules**
**¼ cup minced fresh parsley**
**3 tablespoons ground flaxseeds**
**1 teaspoon paprika**
**1 tablespoon soy sauce**
**2 tablespoons wheat germ**
**¼ cup whole wheat flour**

Combine all of the ingredients in a food processor, or mash in a bowl and mix well.

Preheat the oven to 350°F.

With wet hands, form the mixture into 1-inch balls.

Bake on a lightly oiled cookie sheet for 10 minutes on one side, then roll over and bake 10 more minutes on the other.

Per 2 balls: Calories 112, Protein 5 g, Fat 2 g, Carbohydrates 18 g, Fiber 4 g

# *Curried Black-Eyed Peas*

### Yield: 4 to 6 servings

*Often served in Indian restaurants as channa dal masala, this is a sweet and spicy dish that you'll want to make again and again. It's also good as a cold leftover; you can mash it and use it as a sandwich spread.*

1 large onion, chopped
3 cloves garlic, minced
1 tablespoon minced fresh gingerroot,
  or 1 teaspoon powdered ginger
1 teaspoon canola oil

2 medium potatoes, cut in ½-inch cubes
1 cup chopped fresh or canned tomatoes

2 cups cooked black-eyed peas
⅔ cup bean stock or vegetable broth
4 tablespoons tomato paste
1 cup stewed tomatoes
2 teaspoons curry powder
½ teaspoon salt
¼ teaspoon black pepper
2 tablespoons flax oil

Sauté the onion, garlic, and gingerroot in the canola oil until the onion is transparent.

Add the potatoes and tomatoes, cover, and cook for 5 minutes.

Combine the black-eyed peas, stock, tomato paste, stewed tomatoes, curry powder, salt, and black pepper with the onion/potato mixture; bring to a boil and lower the heat to simmer. Cook for 10 minutes, stirring occasionally. Turn off the heat and stir in the flax oil. Serve over rice or millet.

Per serving: Calories 238, Protein 7 g, Fat 7 g, Carbohydrates 37 g, Fiber 11 g

# *Pat's Baked Beans*

### Yield: 4 servings

*Whip this together and make some potato salad while it's baking. This is a great dish to include in an outdoor meal menu. Be sure the kids are there; they'll love these baked beans.*

**Two 14.5-ounce cans white beans with their juice (3 cups cooked plus 1 cup bean stock)**
**1 teaspoon onion powder, or 1 small onion, diced**
**½ teaspoon garlic granules**
**1 heaping tablespoon yellow mustard**
**¼ cup ketchup**
**⅓ cup molasses**
**¼ cup brown sugar**

**2 tablespoons ground flaxseeds**

Preheat the oven to 300°F.

Mix all of the ingredients together, except the flaxseeds, and bake for 45 minutes in a shallow, 2-quart baking dish until thick but not dry. Remove from the oven and sprinkle the ground flaxseeds over the top before serving.

Per serving: Calories 345, Protein 12 g, Fat 3 g, Carbohydrates 70 g, Fiber 8 g

# Sweet and Sour Tofu

### Yield: 4 servings

*This recipe is just the thing for impressing someone who's never tried tofu.*

1 clove garlic, minced
1 onion, chopped
1 cup chopped celery
1 cup chopped green bell pepper
1 teaspoon oil

1 pound firm tofu, cut into 1-inch cubes
One 20-ounce can unsweetened pineapple chunks
    (Save the juice.)

2 tablespoons cornstarch
¼ teaspoon ground ginger
2 tablespoons soy sauce
¼ cup vinegar
¾ cup pineapple juice
2 tablespoons flax oil

In a 10-inch skillet, sauté the garlic, onion, celery, and green pepper in the oil until soft.

Add the tofu and pineapple to the skillet.

Combine the cornstarch, ginger, soy sauce, vinegar, and pineapple juice in a jar with a tightly fitting lid, and shake vigorously until well mixed. Pour over the tofu/vegetable mixture, and heat until thick, stirring constantly. Gently boil a few minutes. Turn off the heat and stir in the flax oil. Serve over rice.

Per serving: Calories 312, Protein 10 g, Fat 13 g, Carbohydrates 38 g, Fiber 3 g

# Oven–Baked Tofu

### Yield: 20 slices

*This is a kid-pleasing food that's good to have around for quick sandwiches, to have between a split biscuit for a portable breakfast, and cubed to add to a stir fry.*

**½ cup unbleached white flour**
**⅓ cup nutritional yeast**
**2 tablespoons cornmeal**
**3 tablespoons ground flaxseeds**
**1 teaspoon garlic granules**
**½ teaspoon oregano**
**½ teaspoon thyme**

**¼ cup soy sauce**
**¼ cup water**

**2 pounds firm tofu, cut into ¼-inch slices**

In a small, wide bowl, combine the flour, nutritional yeast, cornmeal, flaxseeds, garlic, oregano, and thyme, and mix well.

In another small, wide bowl, combine the soy sauce and water.

Take each slice of tofu (do several at a time), and dip them into the soy sauce bowl, then into the flour mixture bowl. Turn over so each side is coated. Place on a well-oiled cookie sheet. When all the pieces of tofu are dipped and coated and on the baking sheet, sprinkle the remaining flour mixture over the pieces of tofu, and pour the remaining soy sauce over them also. Bake in the lower part of the oven for 20 minutes, or until golden brown. Flip them over with a spatula, and bake for 15 more minutes.

Per serving: Calories 121, Protein 10 g, Fat 6 g, Carbohydrates 10 g, Fiber 1 g

# *Tofu Vegetable Quiche*

### Yield: 8 to 10 servings

*Add some soy bacon bits to this for authentic flavor.*

## *Crust*

1 cup whole wheat pastry flour
1 cup unbleached white flour
1 tablespoon sesame seeds
1 tablespoon ground flaxseeds
½ teaspoon salt
5 tablespoons canola oil
½ cup cold water

## *Filling*

1 large onion, chopped
1 teaspoon canola oil
2 cups snow peas, cut in half
4 ounces mushrooms, sliced

4 cups crumbled firm tofu
   (to be added at different times)
½ cup lemon juice
2 tablespoons soy sauce
1 teaspoon garlic granules
2 tablespoons spicy mustard
4 tablespoons ground flaxseeds
¼ cup nutritional yeast
Paprika, for garnish

This can be baked in a 3-quart, 10-inch-wide, casserole or a 9 x 11-inch glass baking dish. Preheat the oven to 400°F.

To make the crust, mix the flours, seeds, and salt together in a medium mixing bowl. Make a hole in the center, add the 5 tablespoons oil and cold water, and mix. Roll out between layers of wax paper, and place in the baking dish. Crimp the edges to make a pleasant design.

In a medium skillet, sauté the onion in the 1 teaspoon oil until lightly browned. Add the snow peas and cook for 1 minute. Add the canned mushrooms and stir until warmed. Cover and turn off the heat until the blended filling is done.

In a food processor, combine 1 cup of the crumbled tofu, the lemon juice, soy sauce, garlic granules, mustard, and ground flaxseeds. After everything is mixed together, scrape into a mixing bowl. Add the remaining 3 cups crumbled tofu, nutritional yeast, and the sautéed vegetables. Combine well and pour into the prepared pie crust. Sprinkle with paprika. Bake for 15 minutes at 400°F, reduce the heat to 350°F, and bake for 25 more minutes.

Per serving: Calories 312, Protein 14 g, Fat 16 g, Carbohydrates 29 g, Fiber 5 g

# *Stroganoff*

### Yield: 4 to 6 servings

*Textured soy chunks add the perfect chewiness to this dish.*

1 heaping cup textured soy protein chunks
1¾ cups water
2 tablespoons soy sauce
1 teaspoon garlic granules
1 tablespoon balsamic vinegar
4 cups dry pasta (ziti, spirals, or elbows)
1 cup chopped onions
1 teaspoon olive oil
2 cups sliced fresh mushrooms,
      or 4 ounces canned mushrooms
2 cups soymilk
5 tablespoons unbleached white flour
1 teaspoon dried basil
3 tablespoons ground flaxseeds
Salt and pepper, to taste

In a small saucepan, combine the textured soy protein, water, soy sauce, garlic, and vinegar, and bring to a boil. Lower the heat and simmer for 20 minutes.

Cook the pasta al dente.

Meanwhile in a large skillet, sauté the onions in the olive oil until browned. Add the fresh mushrooms and cook until most of the water is cooked out. Add the soymilk, flour, and basil, whisking briskly to stir out any lumps. Cook for 5 minutes, stirring often to develop a smooth sauce. Add the flaxseeds, mushrooms (if using canned ones) and textured soy protein with all its marinade. Season to taste and cook for 1 more minute. Cover until ready to serve over the pasta.

Per serving: Calories 350, Protein 18 g, Fat 7 g, Carbohydrates 60 g, Fiber 7 g

# *Unmeat Loaf*

### Yield: 6 servings

**2 cups textured soy protein granules**
**½ cup ground flaxseeds**
**2 cups boiling water**

**1 medium onion, chopped (¾ cup)**
**½ cup whole wheat flour**
**2 tablespoons tamari**
**1 tablespoon spicy mustard**
**2 teaspoons basil**
**2 teaspoons garlic powder**
**½ teaspoon salt**

In a medium mixing bowl, combine the textured soy protein, flaxseeds, and boiling water, and let rest for 10 minutes.

Preheat the oven to 350°F.

Add the rest of the ingredients to the textured soy protein. Mix well with a spoon or your hands. Press into a lightly oiled bread pan, and bake for 45 minutes. Let cool for 10 minutes before inverting to remove from the pan. Slice and serve with mushroom gravy or salsa.

Per serving: Calories 176, Protein 17 g, Fat 7 g, Carbohydrates 19 g, Fiber 6 g

# Lasagne

### Yield: 6 to 8 servings

*Lasagne without mozzarella and ricotta? Absolutely. Tofu and nutritional yeast provide the perfect combination of light and rich flavors.*

**12 lasagne noodles, cooked and drained**
**6 cups of your favorite seasoned tomato sauce**
**One 13¾-ounce can quartered water-packed artichokes,**
  **(optional)**

### Filling

**3 cups mashed firm tofu**
**3 tablespoons fresh lemon juice**
**1 cup chopped fresh parsley or basil,**
  **or a combination**
**2 tablespoons soy sauce**
**½ cup ground flaxseeds**

### Cheezy Sauce

**1 cup soymilk**
**1 cup water**
**½ cup nutritional yeast flakes**
**4 tablespoons cornstarch**
**1 teaspoon garlic granules**
**⅛ teaspoon turmeric**
**½ teaspoon salt**

Cook the noodles and heat up the tomato sauce while you prepare the filling and cheezy sauce.

To prepare the filling, combine the tofu, lemon juice, parsley, soy sauce, and flaxseeds in a food processor until just mixed but not completely smooth.

To make the cheezy sauce, combine the soymilk, water, nutritional yeast flakes, cornstarch, and spices in a small saucepan. Bring to a boil while stirring. Cook for several minutes, whisking until smooth and thick. Cover until ready to use.

Preheat the oven to 350°F.

Spread 1 cup of the tomato sauce over the bottom of a 9 x 11-inch baking dish. Place 4 of the noodles overlapping to form a layer.

Spoon half of the tofu filling evenly over the noodles. Place the artichoke hearts evenly over the filling, and pour half of the tomato sauce over them. Drizzle ⅓ of the cheezy sauce over the tomato sauce. Layer 4 more noodles followed by the rest of filling. Place the remaining noodles and tomato sauce on top, and pour the remaining cheezy sauce over all in a zig zag pattern.

Bake for 40 to 45 minutes. Remove from the oven and let stand for 10 minutes before serving.

Per serving: Calories 424, Protein 22 g, Fat 11 g, Carbohydrates 63 g, Fiber 11 g

# *Sloppy Joes*

### Yield: 6 servings

*Here's a delicious way to serve tofu that's been frozen and thawed, transforming it from smooth and silky to firm and chewy.*

**1 cup chopped onions**
**3 cloves garlic, minced,**
   **or 1 teaspoon garlic granules**
**1 teaspoon canola oil**

**3 cups water**
**One 6-ounce can tomato paste**
**⅓ cup brown sugar**
**1 tablespoon molasses**
**2 tablespoons soy sauce**
**½ teaspoon allspice**
**½ teaspoon salt**
**1 to 2 crushed red peppers,**
   **or 1 to 1½ teaspoons dried red pepper**
**¼ cup vinegar**

**2 pounds firm tofu, frozen, thawed,**
   **and torn into bite-size pieces**
**3 tablespoons flax oil**

In a large skillet, sauté the onions and garlic in the canola oil until they begin to brown.

Add the water, tomato paste, sugar, molasses, soy sauce, spices, and vinegar to the skillet, and cook for 15 minutes.

Add the tofu pieces to the sauce, and cook for 15 to 20 minutes to let the tofu absorb the flavor of the sauce. Turn off the heat and stir in the flax oil. Serve over sliced whole wheat buns.

Per serving: Calories 322, Protein 18 g, Fat 18 g, Carbohydrates 22 g, Fiber 2 g

# *Great Grain Burgers*

**Yield: 6 to 8 burgers**

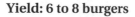

*Grains and flaxseeds make a hearty combination for these tasty, easy burgers.*

**1 small onion, chopped
1 carrot, peeled and grated
1 cup cooked rice, millet, or kasha
1 cup mashed firm tofu
½ cup rolled oats
⅓ cup ground flaxseeds
2 tablespoons soy sauce
1 teaspoon garlic granules
½ teaspoon oregano
Salt and pepper, to taste**

In a medium mixing bowl, combine all the ingredients. Mix well with your hands. Wash your hands and dip them into cold water to prevent the dough from sticking. Form into thin burgers and cook on a lightly oiled skillet until browned on each side.

Per serving: Calories 119, Protein 6 g, Fat 5 g, Carbohydrates 16 g, Fiber 3 g

# Cheyenne's Favorite Veggie Hero

### Yield: 4 sandwiches

*The variety of vegetarian deli items that abound in today's supermarkets make it possible to create a sandwich that would make Dagwood come running.*

**1 loaf French bread**
**2 teaspoons Dijon mustard or mayonnaise**
**2 teaspoons water**
**1 teaspoon flax oil**
**1 tablespoon fresh lemon juice**
**½ teaspoon dried basil**
**½ teaspoon dried oregano**

**½ teaspoon dried marjoram**
**½ teaspoon sea salt**
**2 cups shredded Romaine lettuce**
**1 large cucumber, chopped**
**2 green onions, sliced**
**2 tomatoes, sliced**
**4 slices soy bologna**
**4 slices soy cheddar cheese**
**4 slices soy mozzarella cheese**

Cut the French bread almost in half lengthwise; do not completely cut in half. Spread your favorite mustard or mayonnaise across the top and bottom of the bread, and set aside.

Mix together the water, flax oil, lemon juice, herbs, and salt in a small bowl. Place the lettuce, cucumber, and green onions in a bowl. Pour the lemon juice and flax oil mixture over the veggies, and toss gently. Lay the cheddar cheese across the bottom of the bread. Next arrange the soy bologna, the mozzarella slices, and lettuce/cucumber mixture, and top with the tomatoes. Cut into 4 sandwiches.

Per serving: Calories 261, Protein 16 g, Fat 7 g, Carbohydrates 31 g, Fiber 4 g

# *Veggie–Stuffed Pitas*

**Yield: 4 stuffed pitas**

*Ground flaxseeds add a delicious, nutty flavor to this nutritious sandwich.*

**4 whole-grain pita breads**
**Tofu mayonnaise (optional)**
**1 head broccoli, finely chopped**
**½ head cauliflower, finely chopped**
**½ red cabbage, thinly shredded**
**4 celery stalks, diced**
**4 carrots, shredded**
**Grated soy cheese (optional)**
**Mother Earth's Essential Dressing, page 69**
**4 teaspoons ground flaxseeds**

Slice off an edge of the pita breads to open up the pockets for filling.

Spread the tofu mayonnaise on the sides of the pita breads, if you like. Stuff the pita pockets with the chopped vegetables. If desired, you can top this with grated soy cheese.

Serve the veggie pitas with Mother Earth's Essential Dressing. Top with ground flaxseeds.

Per serving: Calories 216, Protein 8 g, Fat 1 g, Carbohydrates 41 g, Fiber 10 g

# *Baked Oriental Patties*

### Yield: 12 patties

*These patties are delicious served with sweet and sour sauce.*

**1¼ cups chopped onion**
**1 cup chopped green pepper**
**2 teaspoons canola oil**
**1 cup frozen peas**
**4 ounces canned mushrooms**
**5 ounces water chestnuts**
**2 cups mung bean sprouts**
**5 tablespoons ground flaxseeds**

**2 cups firm tofu**
**1 teaspoon garlic powder**
**3 tablespoons tamari**

**1 cup firm tofu**
**¼ cup nutritional yeast**
**⅓ cup unbleached flour**
**2 teaspoons baking powder**

In a medium skillet, sauté the onion and green pepper in the canola oil until soft. Add the peas, mushrooms, and water chestnuts, and stir in until thoroughly heated. Turn off the heat and add the mung bean sprouts and flaxseeds. Cover while you prepare the tofu.

In a food processor, combine the 2 cups tofu, garlic, and tamari until smooth.

Preheat the oven to 400°F.

In a large mixing bowl, mash the 1 cup of tofu along with the nutritional yeast, flour, and baking powder. Add the blended tofu mixture, and the sautéed vegetables, and mix well. Spoon the batter onto 2 cookie sheets. Spread with a spoon to make ½-inch-thick patties about 5 inches across. Bake for 25 minutes until golden brown, flip, and bake for 15 more minutes.

Per pattie: Calories 122, Protein 8 g, Fat 5 g, Carbohydrates 13 g, Fiber 3 g

# Flax-The Super Food

# Side Dishes

# *Seasoned Greens*

### Yield: 10 servings

*This is a great way to enrich your diet with flax oil and vegetables rich in beta carotene.*

**3 pounds kale or collards, steamed**

*Sesame Vinaigrette*

**3 tablespoons flax oil**
**3 tablespoons brown rice vinegar**
**2 tablespoons soy sauce**
**1 teaspoon toasted sesame oil**
**2 tablespoons water**
**1½ teaspoons maple syrup**

Wash the greens thoroughly and drain.

In a large pot, steam the greens for approximately 15 minutes until tender. Remove from the heat and allow to cool until the greens can be handled. Chop up the greens, including the stems. Discard some of the bigger and tougher stems.

In a large mixing bowl, mix together the sesame vinaigrette ingredients. Mix in the chopped greens. This can be served immediately while still warm, later at room temperature, or as a cold dish.

Per serving: Calories 89, Protein 2 g, Fat 5 g, Carbohydrates 10 g, Fiber 4 g

# *Green Beans with Lemon–Garlic Sauce*

**Yield: 4 servings**

*This is also delicious served cold for a summertime picnic.*

**1 pound green beans, ends removed,
    cut into 2-inch pieces**
**1 teaspoon minced garlic**
**⅓ cup fresh lemon juice**
**1 tablespoon soy sauce**
**3 tablespoons ground flaxseeds**

Steam the green beans in ¾ cup water until they are cooked but still firm. Pour out the remaining water, and add the garlic, lemon juice, and soy sauce. Cook over medium heat for 1 minute while stirring. Sprinkle in the ground flaxseeds while stirring. Turn off the heat after the seeds are thoroughly mixed.

Per serving: Calories 66, Protein 3 g, Fat 3 g, Carbohydrates 11 g, Fiber 4 g

# *Fruity Baked Squash or Sweet Potatoes*

**Yield: 4 servings**

*A nutty topping of flaxseeds is the perfect finish to this irresistible combination of sweet vegetables and fruits.*

**2 cups cooked squash (butternut, buttercup, Hubbard, pumpkin) or sweet potatoes**
**½ cup fresh orange juice**
**½ cup chopped dried apricots**
**3 tablespoons ground flaxseeds**
**¼ teaspoon salt**

Preheat the oven to 350°F.

Remove the skin and seeds from the squash, or peel the sweet potatoes. Place in a mixing bowl, and mash with a potato masher. Add the orange juice, apricots, flaxseeds, and salt. Mix well and put into a small lightly oiled baking dish. Cook for 20 minutes.

Per serving: Calories 115, Protein 2 g, Fat 4 g, Carbohydrates 22 g, Fiber 6 g

# Macaroni and Cheeze

### Yield: 6 to 8 servings

*Now you can enjoy this favorite without the dairy. Add small cubes of tofu sautéed in garlic and soy sauce to make a hearty meal.*

**1 pound macaroni or small shells, cooked al dente**

**3 cups water**
**¼ cup cornstarch**
**¼ cup oat flour (grind rolled oats in a blender)**
**1 cup nutritional yeast**
**2 tablespoons spicy mustard**
**1 teaspoon salt**
**⅛ teaspoon turmeric**
**1 teaspoon garlic granules**
**3 tablespoons flax oil**
**1 tablespoon ground flaxseeds**
**¾ cup bread crumbs**

Preheat the oven to 350°F.

Cook the pasta according to package directions.

While the pasta is cooking, prepare the sauce. In a medium saucepan combine the water, cornstarch, oat flour, nutritional yeast, mustard, salt, turmeric, and garlic granules while stirring. Cook, stirring often, over medium heat until the mixture is creamy and starts to bubble. Turn off the heat and mix in the flax oil.

Drain the pasta and pour half of it into a lightly oiled, 3-quart casserole dish. Pour half the cheeze sauce over the noodles, and stir together. Repeat with the remaining pasta and sauce. Sprinkle the flaxseeds and then the bread crumbs over the top. Bake for 30 minutes.

Per serving: Calories 262, Protein 11 g, Fat 8 g, Carbohydrates 36 g, Fiber 1 g

# *Cabbage–Apple Skillet*

### Yield: 6 servings

*This lively dish will fill a wintertime kitchen with wonderful aromas.*

**1 small head cabbage, coarsely chopped
   (6 to 7 cups)
1 teaspoon canola oil
3 cups peeled and chunked apples
Juice of 1 lemon
1 tablespoon poppy seeds
4 tablespoons ground flaxseeds**

In a large skillet, sauté the chopped cabbage in the oil.

Add the apple chunks to the cooking cabbage. Cover and cook, stirring occasionally, for about 5 minutes until the cabbage and apples are soft but not mushy. Add the lemon juice, poppy seeds, and flaxseeds. Stir, cover, and cook for 1 minute, then turn off the heat. Let stand for a few minutes, and stir again before serving.

Per serving: Calories 101, Protein 2 g, Fat 4 g, Carbohydrates 19 g, Fiber 5 g

# *Knishes*

**Yield: Thirty-four 3-inch knishes**

*These little flax-rich potato rolls are the ultimate comfort food.*

### Dough
    1½ cups mashed potatoes
    ½ teaspoon salt
    3 tablespoons ground flaxseeds
    1 cup whole wheat pastry flour
    2 cups unbleached white flour
    2 tablespoons canola oil
    7 tablespoons cold water

### Filling
    1¾ cups finely chopped onions
    1 teaspoon olive oil
    2½ cups mashed potatoes
    2 tablespoons ground flaxseeds
    1 teaspoon salt
    ⅛ teaspoon black pepper

In a medium mixing bowl, combine the 1½ cups mashed potatoes, ½ teaspoon salt, and 3 tablespoons flaxseeds. Add the flours, canola oil, and water.

To make the filling, cook the onions in the olive oil until browned. Combine them in a bowl with the 2½ cups mashed potatoes, 2 tablespoons flaxseeds, salt, and pepper.

Preheat the oven to 350°F.

Divide the dough in half. Roll out each half on a lightly floured surface until it is thin. Cut across and down to make 3½ x 3-inch rectangles. Place a heaping tablespoon of filling in a long thin line down the middle of each piece of cut dough. Fold up the ends and roll up so you can pinch to seal the edges. Place on a cookie sheet about 1 inch apart, and bake for 20 minutes.

Per serving: Calories 132, Protein 3 g, Fat 3 g, Carbohydrates 24 g, Fiber 3 g

# *Spaghetti Balls*

### Yield: 10 balls

*Serve these with your favorite marina sauce for a dish your kids will find irresistible.*

**1 cup textured soy protein granules**
**⅞ cup boiling water**

**½ teaspoon garlic powder**
**½ teaspoon oregano**
**½ teaspoon cumin**
**½ teaspoon salt**
**1 tablespoon flax oil**
**2 tablespoons ground flaxseeds**
**¼ cup unbleached white flour**

In a medium mixing bowl, soak the textured soy protein in the water for 10 minutes.

Add the rest of the ingredients, and mix well.

Form into 1-inch balls. Brown in a lightly oiled skillet, rolling around to cook all sides, or bake on a cookie sheet, turning several times to brown on several sides.

Per ball: Calories 54, Protein 5 g, Fat 3 g, Carbohydrates 5 g, Fiber 1 g

# Flax-The Super Food

# Desserts

# *Apple Cobbler*

### Yield: 6 servings

*Try this a la mode with a scoop of vanilla nondairy frozen dessert.*

### Apple Mixture

  6 cups chopped apples (peeling is optional)
  3 tablespoons lemon juice
  ½ cup raw or brown sugar
  ½ teaspoon cinnamon
  ¼ teaspoon nutmeg

### Cobbler

  1 cup unbleached white flour
  ¾ cup oat flour (grind rolled oats in a blender)
  ¼ teaspoon salt
  1½ teaspoons baking powder

  2½ tablespoons flaxseeds
  ⅔ cup warm water
  ½ cup liquid sweetener
  ½ teaspoon vanilla
  ⅓ cup soymilk

Preheat the oven to 375°F.

Mix the apples, lemon juice, sugar, cinnamon, and nutmeg together in a medium mixing bowl, and pour into a deep, lightly oiled 2-quart baking dish.

In the same bowl that you mixed the apples in, combine the flour, blended oats, salt, and baking powder.

Combine the flaxseeds, water, sweetener, vanilla, and soymilk together in a blender until smooth; add to the dry ingredients. Stir together until all the dry ingredients are absorbed. Pour over the top of the apples, and spread evenly around to the edges. Bake for 40 to 45 minutes. This is good served hot or cold.

Per serving: Calories 260, Protein 5 g, Fat 2 g, Carbohydrates 53 g, Fiber 7 g

# *Oatmeal Cookies Supreme*

### Yield: 3 dozen cookies

*Make lots of these fruit- and nut-filled cookies—they disappear quickly.*

1½ tablespoons flaxseeds
½ cup warm water
¼ cup sesame oil
¾ cup sorghum molasses

### *Dry ingredients*

1½ cups rolled oats
1½ cups unbleached white flour
½ teaspoon salt
1 teaspoon baking soda
1 teaspoon cinnamon
¼ teaspoon cloves

½ cup chopped dried apricots or dates or figs (optional)
½ cup chopped pecans or walnuts (optional)

Preheat the oven to 350°F.

Process the flaxseeds with the warm water in a blender until the consistency is smooth and creamy and the seeds are broken up into small, dark flecks. In a medium mixing bowl, blend the flaxseed mixture, oil, and molasses together with a whisk.

Add the dry ingredients and mix everything together very well. Add the chopped fruit and nuts, and mix.

Place by heaping teaspoons on a lightly oiled cookie sheet, and bake for 10 minutes.

Per cookie: Calories 69, Protein 1 g, Fat 2 g, Carbohydrates 12 g, Fiber 1 g

# *Crescent Poppy Seed Cookies*

### Yield: 24 cookies

*These pastry-style cookies are favorites for teas and parties.*

### *Dough*

    1½ tablespoons flaxseeds
    ½ cup warm water
    1½ cups flour
    ¼ teaspoon salt
    2 teaspoons baking powder
    2 tablespoons oil or nonhydrogenated,
        nondairy margarine
    ⅓ cup sugar
    ½ teaspoon grated lemon zest

    6 tablespoons liquid sweetener
    3 tablespoons poppy seeds

Process the flaxseeds with the warm water in a blender until the consistency is smooth and creamy and the seeds are broken up into small, dark flecks.

With a wooden spoon, mix the flaxseed mixture together with the flour, salt, baking powder, oil, sugar, and lemon zest. The dough should be stiff but soft. Put the dough in the refrigerator to chill for 1 hour.

Divide the chilled dough into 3 parts. Make a ball with the first part, and roll it out into a circle about 9 inches in diameter (just as thinly as you can roll it and not have the dough break apart). Return the other 2 parts to the refrigerator to continue chilling while you roll out the first ball.

Drizzle the 2 tablespoons of the liquid sweetener and 1 tablespoon of the poppy seeds over the round dough, and cut it into 6 pie-shaped wedges. Loosen the dough from the counter with a spatula. Roll up each piece, beginning with the wide edge and ending with the point rolled up on the outside center of the cookie, like a croissant. Slightly bend each cookie into a crescent as you place it on a baking sheet. Repeat the same procedure with the other 2 parts of the dough.

Bake the cookies for 10 minutes at 350°F.

Remove the cookies from the pan after they have cooled.

Per serving: Calories 70, Protein 1 g, Fat 2 g, Carbohydrates 13 g, Fiber 0 g

# *Easy Chocolate Chip Cookies*

Yield: 32 cookies

*Flaxseeds add moistness and nutrition to these best-loved cookies.*

### *Liquid ingredients*

1½ tablespoons flaxseeds
½ cup warm water
3 tablespoons sesame oil
1 teaspoon vanilla
½ cup liquid sweetener
4 tablespoons plain soy yogurt

### *Dry ingredients*

¼ teaspoon salt
2 cups unbleached white flour
1 teaspoon baking soda

2 cups (12-ounces) semi-sweet chocolate chips

Preheat the oven to 350°F.

Process the flaxseeds with the warm water in a blender until the consistency is smooth and creamy and the seeds are broken up into small, dark flecks. In a medium mixing bowl, combine the flaxseed mixture with the remaining liquid ingredients. Add the dry ingredients to the liquid ingredients to make a soft batter.

Add the chocolate chips and mix well. Drop by tablespoonfuls onto a cookie sheet, and bake for 10 minutes.

Per cookie: Calories 94, Protein 1 g, Fat 5 g, Carbohydrates 11 g, Fiber 1 g

# *Chocolate Cake*

### Yield: 10 to 12 servings

*Now you can have your cake, and eat more healthfully too.*

**Liquid ingredients**

 3 tablespoons flaxseeds
 ¾ cup warm water
 ⅓ cup sesame oil
 1 teaspoon vanilla
 2 cups soymilk

**Dry ingredients**

 2½ cups unbleached white flour
 ⅔ cup cocoa
 1 cup sugar
 2 teaspoons baking soda
 ½ teaspoon salt

Preheat the oven to 350°F.

Process the flaxseeds with the warm water in a blender until the consistency is smooth and creamy and the seeds are broken up into small, dark flecks. In a medium mixing bowl, mix the flaxseed mixture with the remaining liquid ingredients

Sift the dry ingredients into the bowl of liquid ingredients, and beat until smooth.

Pour the well-beaten batter into two 9-inch cake pans that have been lightly oiled. Bake for 25 to 30 minutes, or until a toothpick inserted in the center comes out clean. Cool and spread with your favorite frosting.

Per serving: Calories 260, Protein 6 g, Fat 8 g, Carbohydrates 40 g, Fiber 4 g

# *Surprise Bundt Cake*

### Yield: 12 servings

*This cake is as much fun to eat as it is to make.*

### *Surprise filling*

3 tablespoons nonhydrogenated,
    nondairy margarine
⅔ cup brown sugar
1 tablespoon flour
2 teaspoons cinnamon
1 cup chopped nuts
½ cup raisins

### *Liquid ingredients*

3 tablespoons flaxseeds
¾ cup warm water
¼ cup sesame oil
1 cup plain soy yogurt
1 cup liquid sweetener
1 teaspoon vanilla

### *Dry ingredients*

3 cups flour
2 teaspoons baking powder
1 teaspoon baking soda
½ teaspoon salt

Preheat the oven to 350°F.

In a small mixing bowl, combine the ingredients for the surprise filling, and set aside.

Process the flaxseeds with the warm water in a blender until the consistency is smooth and creamy and the seeds are broken up into small, dark flecks. In a medium mixing bowl, mix the flaxseed mixture with the remaining liquid ingredients for the cake batter. Sift the dry ingredients into the liquid ingredients, and beat well until smooth.

Pour ⅓ of the cake batter into an oiled bundt pan. Smooth out the batter so it is level. With your hands or a large spoon, sprinkle all the filling over the cake batter in the cake pan, and even it up. Pour the remaining batter over the filling, and spread out to the edges of the pan so the filling is entirely covered with batter. Bake for 45 minutes. Let cool, then remove from the pan. Drip a lemon glaze over the top or eat plain.

Per serving: Calories 384, Protein 5 g, Fat 13 g, Carbohydrates 58 g, Fiber 3 g

# No-Cook Nut Balls

### Yield: 14 balls

*This is a quick and easy snack that takes minutes to make and requires no baking. It's a tasty treat that even kids can make themselves. Great for the holidays!*

**¼ cup natural peanut butter**
**¼ cup liquid sweetener**
**1 teaspoon flax oil**
**2 tablespoons carob chips**
**¼ cup chopped walnuts**
**1 cup brown rice crispies**

In a medium mixing bowl, mix together the peanut butter, liquid sweetener, and flax oil.

Add the carob chips, walnuts, and rice crispies. Mix gently until the crispies are well coated.

Cover a large plate or container with wax paper. To make the balls, dip your hands in a bowl of water and form the mixture into walnut-sized balls.

Refrigerate to chill.

*Variation ideas: Spread the mixture out in a pan, and use a cookie cutter, such as a heart shape, to cut out shapes. Decorate if desired. Another fun idea is to oil a muffin tin and shape the mixture into the individual muffin cups. Chill. When ready to serve fill the cups with your favorite frozen non-dairy ice cream. Stick in a candle for fun birthday cups, and decorate if desired. You can even fill these cups with your favorite pudding.*

Per ball: Calories 77, Protein 2 g, Fat 4 g, Carbohydrates 9 g, Fiber 0 g

# *Milky Way Dunking and Dipping Sauce*

**Yield: 1 cup**

*Make fruit kabobs by alternating pieces of strawberries, grapes, pineapple, apples, star fruit, and melon on wooden skewers, and serve this sauce on the side.*

**1 cup vanilla soy yogurt**
**¼ cup plain soy yogurt**
**1 cup soy sour cream**
**2 tablespoons plus 2 teaspoons maple syrup**
**1 teaspoon flax oil**
**Fresh whole strawberries, apple slices,**
    **pineapple chunks, etc.**

In a medium mixing bowl, mix the yogurts, sour cream, maple syrup, and flax oil.

Chill and serve with your favorite fresh fruit.

Per tablespoon of sauce without fruit: Calories 49, Protein 1 g, Fat 2 g, Carbohydrates 5 g, Fiber 0 g

# Sweet Potato Pie

### Yield: 8 servings

*Flax in both the crust and filling of this pie makes it a nutritional powerhouse of a dessert.*

## Crust

½ cup whole wheat flour
1 cup unbleached flour
2 tablespoons ground flaxseeds
¼ teaspoon salt
3 tablespoons canola oil
6 to 7 tablespoons cold water

## Filling

1½ cups warm soymilk
1½ cups mashed sweet potatoes
3 tablespoons ground flaxseeds
1 teaspoon cinnamon
½ teaspoon allspice
¼ teaspoon ground cloves
½ teaspoon salt
¼ cup molasses
½ cup maple syrup

Preheat the oven to 400°F.

Combine the crust ingredients in a mixing bowl. Roll out the dough between 2 sheets of wax paper. Press the dough into a 9-inch pie pan, and crimp the edges.

Combine the filling ingredients in a food processor or in batches in a blender until smooth. Pour into the prepared pie shell.

Bake for 15 minutes. Lower the heat to 350°F, and bake for 30 more minutes.

Cool before serving.

Per serving: Calories 289, Protein 5 g, Fat 9 g, Carbohydrates 51 g, Fiber 3 g

# Index

## A

## B

## C

# Meet the Authors

Barb Bloomfield *(Soups On!, Fabulous Beans)* is an acclaimed cook from The Farm, America's largest vegetarian community, where she runs a vegetarian bed and breakfast, and is a recipe editor for Book Publishing Company.

Judy Brown *(The Natural Lunchbox, Judy Brown's Guide to Natural Foods Cooking)* holds a MS in

Consumer Economics and has been active in the natural foods industry for 22 years. She has worked in public relations & marketing for natural food products, conducted cooking classes and demonstrations, written articles for publications including *Whole Foods, Well Being Journal* and *Body, Mind, Spirit,* and is well-known as a consumer educator and lecturer.

No one knows flax better than Siegfried Gursche. At various points in his career he has developed, marketed, and distributed flax products for the health food market and studied flax farming and pressing techniques the world over. He is the founder and publisher of *alive* magazine and *alive* books and is the author of *Healing with Herbal Juices.*

127

Purchase these informative vegetarian cookbooks from your local bookstore or natural foods store, or you can buy them directly from:

Book Publishing Company
P.O. Box 99
Summertown, Tn 38483
1-800-695-2241
www.bookpubco.com

Delicious Food for
a Healthy Heart
$12.95

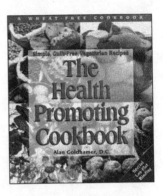

The Health
Promoting
Cookbook
$12.95

Warming Up to
Living Foods
$15.95

The Magic
of Soy
$9.95

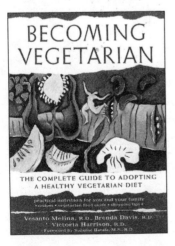

Becoming
Vegetarian
$15.95

Soyfoods Cooking
for a Positive
Menopause
$12.95

Please include $3.50 per book for shipping.